‖‖‖ ‖‖‖‖ ‖ ‖‖‖‖ ‖‖ ‖‖ ‖‖‖ ‖‖‖‖ ‖‖‖
D1714876

LEADING WOMEN

Lena Dunham

Feminist Writer, Actor, Producer, and Director

KAITLYN DULING

Cavendish Square

New York

Published in 2018 by Cavendish Square Publishing, LLC
243 5th Avenue, Suite 136, New York, NY 10016

Copyright © 2018 by Cavendish Square Publishing, LLC

First Edition

Website: cavendishsq.com

This publication represents the opinions and views of the author based on his or her personal experience, knowledge, and research. The information in this book serves as a general guide only. The author and publisher have used their best efforts in preparing this book and disclaim liability rising directly or indirectly from the use and application of this book.

All websites were available and accurate when this book was sent to press.

Library of Congress Cataloging-in-Publication Data

Names: Duling, Kaitlyn, author.
Title: Lena Dunham : feminist writer, actor, producer, and director / Kaitlyn Duling.
Description: New York : Cavendish Square Publishing, 2018. | Series: Leading women | Includes bibliographical references and index.
Identifiers: LCCN 2017015926 (print) | LCCN 2017029290 (ebook) | ISBN 9781502631770 (E-book) | ISBN 9781502631763 (library bound) | ISBN 9781502634146 (pbk.)
Subjects: LCSH: Dunham, Lena, 1986- | Television producers and directors--United States--Biography. | Actors--United States--Biography.
Classification: LCC PN1992.4.D86 (ebook) | LCC PN1992.4.D86 D85 2018 (print) | DDC 791.4502/8092 [B] --dc23
LC record available at https://lccn.loc.gov/2017015926

Editorial Director: David McNamara
Editor: Jodyanne Benson
Copy Editor: Nathan Heidelberger
Associate Art Director: Amy Greenan
Designer: Renni Johnson
Production Coordinator: Karol Szymczuk
Photo Research: J8 Media

The photographs in this book are used by permission and through the courtesy of: Cover Noam Galai/WireImage/Getty Images; p. 1 Reuters/Alamy Stock Photo; p. 4 Seth Poppel Yearbook Library; p. 7 Ben Gabbe/Getty Images for Tribeca Film Festival; p. 9 Andrew Toth/Getty Images; p. 16 David Livingston/WireImage/Getty Images; p. 25 Philip Scalia/Alamy Stock Photo; p. 27 Michael Buckner/Getty Images for SXSW; p. 30 John W. Ferguson/Getty Images; p. 33 AF Archive/Alamy Stock Photo; p. 37 John W. Ferguson/Getty Images; p. 40 Bryan Bedder/Getty Images for The New Yorker; p. 42 Jason Merritt/Getty Images; p. 46 Collection Christophel/Alamy Stock Photo; p. 49 HBO Album/Newscom; p. 55 Gardiner Anderson/Bauer-Griffin/GC Images/Getty Images; p. 60 Zuma Press/Alamy Stock Photo; p. 64 Jamie McCarthy/Getty Images; p. 69 Randy Shropshire/Getty Images for Planned Parenthood Los Angeles; p. 75 Mike Coppola/Getty Images; p. 77 Stephen Lovekin/Getty Images for Point Foundation; p. 80 Stuart C. Wilson/Getty Images; p. 90 Jamie McCarthy/Getty Images; p. 93 Angela Weiss/AFP/Getty Images.

Printed in the United States of America

CONTENTS

CHAPTER ONE

Introduction to Lena Dunham

Early Years

Lena Dunham has never been good at keeping secrets. Whether it was her own tales from school, the details of her friends' lives, or even intimate family information, Dunham has always loved to tell stories. Throughout her youngest years, she shared secrets with anyone and everyone she could find—strangers in the grocery store, teachers, friends. As she grew up, that passion for sharing led her to study the arts. Storytelling, merged with her skills in writing and directing, became a distinct professional path that she could follow and build upon. Dunham has never shied away from who she is

Since her youngest years, Lena Dunham has been telling stories and creating art that reflects her life.

at her core—a sharer who is in love with telling other people's stories, as well as her own, not to mention a wry comedian who is determined to break down assumptions about who she is and who she should be.

Lena Dunham was born on May 13, 1986, in New York City. Raised in Manhattan, her childhood was New York City through and through. She has said the city is "in my gut like an old sickness."[1] She rode the subway with her parents and delighted in the pigeons who scattered on the sidewalks, the tall buildings, the crowds of people. Outside, it was constant noise, and inside her head, just as loud. She was born into a family of artists. Her mother, Laurie Simmons, is a photographer, and her dad, Carroll Dunham, a painter. Simmons has worked primarily with dolls and dollhouses, photographing scenes created on a miniature scale that feature carefully set interiors and doll figures. Her husband's work is eclectic, including drawings, paintings, and sculptures on various subjects. Lena has jokingly referred to her mom as a "Long Island Jew" and her dad as a "Connecticut WASP," though there is surely much more to them than that![2] "WASP" is an old descriptor that stands for "white Anglo-Saxon Protestant." True, Lena's mother was Jewish, and her father was Protestant. As a child, she grew up engaged with both religious traditions, celebrating Christmas and Hanukkah, attending neither church nor synagogue on the weekends. Dunham has said that she feels culturally Jewish, and she is often cited as a celebrity who hails from the Jewish tradition.

Lena's parents, Laurie (*right*) and Carroll (*left*) are both artists.

Active professional artists, her parents raised Lena in Manhattan. She has always had a passion for cabdrivers, believing them to be the most brilliant people on the planet. In second grade, Lena told her classmates that her father was a cabdriver, though he had only driven cabs for a few months, over ten years before Lena was born! Due to her parents' busy schedules and their unique home life, Lena and her sister grew up eating a variety of takeout— Chinese and Indian and all manner of interesting foods—for dinner each night, usually gathered on the floor around the coffee table. Her parents were present, often immersing their children in the art world, taking them to gallery openings and holding parties, full of artists and eclectic individuals, at their home.

For six years, Lena enjoyed all the pleasures and triumphs of being raised as an only child. She wanted siblings, though, and as a preschooler she went so far as to tell her teacher that her mother was expecting! Learning of the lie, her parents began to try for another child. When they announced to Lena that she would be a big sister, she emphatically stated, "I changed my mind."[3] However, as they grew up together, Lena came to deeply love and appreciate her little sister. She has praised her sister's bright intellect and has always been intrigued by the parts of her that are, according to Lena, "unknowable." Their relationship, though challenging, is full and extremely important to both of them. When she was seventeen, Grace came out to Lena as a lesbian. Lena began to cry, not out of unhappiness but because it became clear how little she truly knew about Grace. Unfortunately, due to her inability to keep her mouth shut, Lena was the one who revealed Grace's secret to her mother, damaging the trusting relationship she'd built with Grace and confusing and upsetting her parents in the process. "Basically, it's like I can't keep any of my own secrets," Lena told the *New York Times*. "And I consider Grace to be an extension of me, and therefore I couldn't handle the fact that she's a very private person."[4] As the only two children in their family, Grace and Lena were very close, and they have remained close throughout life. Grace graduated from Brown University and became a gender-nonconforming activist. Grace and Lena are in constant, friendly debate. They text or FaceTime each and every day, keeping each other informed and engaged in nearly every aspect of their lives.

Lena's younger sister, Grace, has joined Lena on the red carpet on several occasions.

Obsessive-Compulsive Disorder

While Lena's childhood, one of **privilege** and comfort, was full of positive experiences that helped mold her into the high achiever she is today, many of her earliest years are marked by struggles with mental health. **Obsessive-compulsive disorder**, challenging relationships with food, and other issues have plagued Dunham from her elementary years into adulthood. At age nine, she began seeing a therapist, working her way through several different professionals before she found one who could best help her cope, both on a daily basis and with her mental health problems as a whole. Though she had exhibited the behaviors for quite a long time, Dunham was diagnosed with obsessive-compulsive disorder at age eleven. This disorder is marked by compulsions that are very difficult to control, and it can manifest itself differently in each individual. Over the years, Dunham has used medication to help her control these behaviors, which have ranged from food-related compulsions to physical movements and rituals. Throughout her childhood, Dunham's life was marked by a long list of fears: diseases, certain foods, headaches, kidnapping, sleep. As she grew older, her mental health issues became a concern to her parents. Dunham insisted on inspecting every food item in the house and worried constantly about death, diseases, and disasters.

Dunham's parents, no strangers to therapy, decided to find their young daughter a therapist of her own, in order to help her work through some of her challenges. Both Laurie and Carroll had therapists of their own, and Lena herself has kept up with therapy, in various forms, for most of her life. While her mental health issues and obsessive-compulsive disorder will likely never disappear altogether, she has learned to live a productive and happy life alongside her struggles with germophobia (fear of germs), hypochondria (fear of diseases), and other concerns.

School Years

Dunham went to Saint Ann's School in Brooklyn. Throughout her entire education, she did not enjoy school. In fact, following her first day of kindergarten, she declared to her father, "It was fun, but I don't think

I'll go back."[5]. She didn't have many friends at all, and she has always been unsure if this was by choice or by circumstance. In seventh grade, when she shifted to a Quaker school, she had some of her best educational experiences. The school allowed her to write poems, create plays, engage in lively debates, and, ultimately, express herself creatively and authentically. Her memories of these years are bright. She was close with her sister and, though she didn't have many friends, collected a number of pets. Grace and Lena, over the years, shared an iguana, a rabbit, two turtles, two gerbils, three cats, and a dog! It is easy to imagine Lena acting out stories with her pets, talking to them, sharing secrets, and pretending they were human companions. Much of Lena's childhood was spent alone in her room, talking to her pets, making scrapbooks, watching television, and learning to enjoy her solitude.

"I was a bona fide weirdo in high school," says Dunham.[6] As she grew into her teenage years, she skipped over many of the traditional markers of teen life. She failed her driver's test and never received her license. In fact, she still doesn't have a license to drive and doesn't plan on getting one anytime soon. In New York City, it is easy to ride the subway around the city—ducking down under the bustling street, boarding the train, racing off across the world, and then emerging, popping back up into the bitter cold (or extremely hot and sticky, depending on the season) air, at just the destination you had imagined. She didn't excel in academics or social life. Four years of

Dog Lover

The definitive source about her own childhood, Lena Dunham has described how her greatest dream as a child was to find a box full of puppies. In a piece for the *New Yorker* titled "A Box of Puppies," Dunham mapped out her lifelong desire for a square container filled with small, new, wriggling canines. She made up names for them (Anastasia and Kristy) and prepped for the day when she could walk down the street with them, no leash necessary, queen of SoHo and of puppies.

When she was fifteen, Dunham discovered the concept of fostering—taking in dogs for a temporary period of time. At the suggestion of an animal-rescue group she met on the sidewalk, she took in three pit bull puppies, just days old, and didn't tell her parents, who were on a trip to California. All weekend, she cared for the puppies to the point of near obsession. But when her parents returned from California and discovered them, the three were immediately returned. No more box full of puppies.

As she grew older, Dunham still hoped for a dog. When she moved out on her own, she still wanted one, but her boyfriend, Jack Antonoff, is allergic to dogs. After much waiting and thinking, she reenacted the "box of puppies" scenario from her childhood. She waited until Antonoff was gone, traveled to a rescue center, and brought home a dog. Her mutt, Lamby, became her best canine friend and a much-loved member of her family. Though Dunham never got the cardboard box full of puppies she wanted, her dog dreams have, to some extent, come true.

high school was four years too long for Dunham. In an interview with *Rookie* magazine, Dunham said, "I still have nightmares that I'm stuck in high school again."[7] During these years, she didn't feel pretty, and she didn't have a boyfriend, though she wanted one. In fact, during her high school years, she got in trouble for punching boys! When she talks in the press about being a "weirdo," especially in publications geared toward teens and young adults, Dunham loudly pronounces the benefits of weirdo life. To **assimilate**, or conform to the conventions that are expected of young people—specific clothes, makeup, behaviors, etc.—is not Dunham's vision for a full or positive life. She encourages all people to embrace their uniqueness. This is an issue that has continued to be close to her heart throughout her relatively short career and life.

Luckily, high school doesn't last forever! After slogging through her many years of compulsory— required—education, Dunham made her way to college. She first arrived at the New School, located in Manhattan, where her parents lived and where she grew up. Dunham enjoyed many moments at the New School, but her experience there didn't align with her vision of the ideal college experience. She explains, "There were a lot of kids who were really excited to have just gotten to New York … They wanted to go to clubs or go to Broadway."[8] After two semesters there, she transferred to Oberlin College, a small, well-known liberal arts college in Oberlin, Ohio. Oberlin was everything New York City was not—quiet, rural, midwestern, and small. Dunham expected herself to flourish there, and she did, in her own way. At first, she was a star student, showing up early to each class with a cup of tea in her hand, writing down due dates and notes in her journal. But about a month into each semester, she would slide back into old patterns of lateness, disinterest, and all the markers of "slogging through" that had made up her high school experience.

In her junior year of college, Dunham met her first love—Noah. Though she had been friends, and sometimes more than friends, with many men throughout college, Noah was her first serious relationship. Dunham has referred to Noah as, "arguably the only man I've ever truly loved," until her current partner, Jack Antonoff.[9] Though they only dated for a year and a half, their relationship felt, to Dunham, like a fifty-year love story. She was interested in him completely, head-over-heels for all of his quirks, interests, and fashions. A cinema-studies student, many of Noah's own passions aligned with hers, and his unique personality drew her to him. After a few months, they were inseparable. Dunham says of Noah: "I told him I hoped we would die at the same time in the mouth of a lion."[10] Their breakup, after she graduated, would be messy and complex (as can be expected at the end of a passionate first relationship). Dunham has often reflected, in writing, about her time with him, and about what the relationship meant to her.

Filmmaking

While she did find some positive outlets during her time at Oberlin, such as short filmmaking and writing, she never quite enjoyed herself or flourished as much as she expected she would. She took many naps, she kept journals, and she explored her sexuality. A simple YouTube search reveals a few of the independent films Dunham produced while in college. Most of these films fell into the **mumblecore** genre, characterized by low-budget production, **improvisation**, naturalistic dialogue, and a focus on the relationships of young adults. The genre has been active since the early 2000s. Dunham released *Pressure* in 2006, filmed on the floor of the Oberlin College library. Just a few minutes long and featuring only three actresses, *Pressure* was her first foray into short film, and she quickly grew to love the medium. In 2007, she produced *The Fountain*, a six-minute film featuring Dunham in a bikini, brushing her teeth in a public fountain. Instead of going to film school, Dunham developed her own practice of writing and producing tiny, flawed sketches of life that she uploaded to the internet. Her films touched on themes she would later dive into in her feature-length films and television show: sexuality, entitlement, and **millennial** culture. Though at the time the short films may have felt like a fun hobby, they would ultimately become the stepping stones to a fully developed career in television and film.

CHAPTER TWO

Early Successes in Filmmaking

Between the stumbles and attempts of her college years and the eventual runaway success of *Girls*, Dunham took time to explore and expand her creative interests, producing work that would gain her some notoriety, if not the hit-out-of-the-ballpark achievements every artist dreams of. While her earliest short films gained her some popularity and notoriety on campus, they never went **viral**, circulating rapidly on the internet. Instead, those forays into moviemaking allowed Dunham to get her feet wet in the writing, directing, producing, and acting worlds—all at once!

Dunham got her start in filmmaking at an early age, while she was still in college.

Triple Threat

Dunham has long been a "triple threat," or even more, as she has the skill sets for a number of different jobs related to moviemaking. Since childhood, she has enjoyed writing, first becoming enamored with it in middle school. When she was finally encouraged to write poetry and plays, her brain couldn't stop creating. After slogging through high school and her exciting, but not exactly inspirational, years at Oberlin College, Dunham moved back to New York City to live in a small room at the back of her parents' loft.

While she hoped to write, create, and eventually make more films, Dunham's life was characterized, at this time, by disappointment. The disappointment of her parents **pervaded** the apartment. She herself was embarrassed by the fact that she paid no rent, ate food provided by her parents, and slept in until noon each day. Once outside of the structure of college, Dunham felt lost at sea, swimming in her far-off dreams and goals but not actually getting anywhere.

Eventually, after months of the unemployed, bored existence, Dunham reconnected with her old friends from preschool, Isabel and Joana. The three friends had all recently landed back in Tribeca after finishing up their respective degrees. Without much direction among them, Dunham and Joana found a glimmer of productivity by working retail at the upscale children's clothing boutique where Isabel worked, Peach and the Babke. Each day, she sold grown-up fashions for pint-size customers, often at exorbitant prices, and giggled about the customers with her coworkers. This was her first experience with "adulting," making her way in the world without the structure of school or childhood to protect and guide her, and it was, as most experiences in Dunham's life, not quite the norm. The boutique's staff enjoyed free lunches, short shifts, and low expectations. Dunham and her friends made use of their extra time and cash by enjoying everything New York City's art world had to offer, following in the footsteps of their parents by attending gallery shows, openings, and events across the city. It was during this time that Dunham would have many of the experiences—with dating, friendships, family, and the city itself—that she would later mine for her television shows and movies.

Tight Shots

Eventually, those short, uneventful (save for the celebrities who would occasionally drop in) shifts at the children's boutique would lose their luster, and Dunham would begin to search for artistic challenges. In 2007, while still in college, she produced a ten-episode web series for Nerve called *Tight Shots*. Writer L. V. Anderson, in a piece for *Slate*, watched everything Dunham ever directed. After consuming the entire collection, she dubbed the series the "best of [Dunham's] early work."[1]

Tight Shots, like much of Dunham's work, dealt with subject matter she was familiar with: student filmmaking aspirations. She played the main character, also named Lena, who was attempting to produce her first film.

The series introduced, in a big way, two subjects that would feature prominently in her later work: boorish boyfriends and on-screen sexuality. As her experience grew, Dunham returned to these topics again and again, making screen time for discussions of bodies, relationships, and gender that were not, and are still not, given ample space in television and movies. Nerve has since brought the show back, featuring it on their website in advance of the premiere of *Girls.* Many of those she collaborated with in *Tight Shots* would eventually find places in Dunham's other projects. As Dunham developed her style across shows and films, she would return, again and again, to the themes and actors that appeared in these first projects, threading them as a constant throughout her lifetime body of work.

Delusional Downtown Divas

After graduation, Dunham launched a low-budget web series, commissioned (ordered) by *Index* magazine, a publication focusing on arts and culture in New York City. Dubbed *Delusional Downtown Divas* and premiering in 2009, the series depicted three women of questionable talent attempting to make their way in the art world. Dunham played Oona, an aspiring novelist, while her friend Isabel Halley took on the part of AgNess, a businesswoman, and Joana Avillez brought life to Swann, a performance artist. The show was meant to be a satire or parody of the New York City art world, but it attracted a **cult following**, a particular section of society that deemed it fashionable, enjoyable, and popular.

The comedy web series, an unpaid project, lasted for two seasons, or twenty episodes total. It earned the attention of artists and critics such as Yvonne Force Villareal, Nate Lowman, Rob Pruitt, and Deborah Kass, some of whom appeared in the show. Dunham directed the episodes, each just under ten minutes. With shaking camera work, near-constant dialogue, and a lo-fi feel, *Delusional Downtown Divas* wasn't a far cry from Dunham's mumblecore days. The show revolved around the three main characters' attempts to make their way in the New York art world, an environment that Dunham had grown up in and, as a film director and resident of New York City, explored on her own as a young adult. "The characters are definitely versions of us," Dunham told *New York Magazine*.[2] The characters in *Delusional Downtown Divas* were just that—delusional. The jokes were primarily at the expense of the characters, and it is difficult (perhaps impossible) for the viewer to feel sympathy toward the three women in their clueless, desperate attempts to gain fame and fortune through art.

After watching the first few episodes, conceptual artist Rob Pruitt invited Dunham, Halley, and Avillez

Lena Dunham

Viral Video vs. Short Film

If you've spent any amount of time on the internet, especially on Facebook, you've probably encountered a number of "viral videos," clips that are shared rapidly and widely around the web. These videos, usually lasting just seconds or a few minutes, often have extremely clickable titles that describe what will happen in the short. Whether it's a baby being cute, an animal dancing, or a slow-motion car crash, these videos can gain immense popularity over a number of hours or days, thanks, in part, to social media sites like Facebook and Twitter that make it easy to share media with large, diverse networks of people.

When Dunham set out, at Oberlin, to make short films, she wasn't hoping to make "viral videos." Though her films (*Pressure*, *Open the Door,* and *The Fountain,* among others) were each just a few minutes long, and though they were uploaded and shared through YouTube, they did not have many of the characteristics that make videos "go viral," such as extreme bursts of comedy, music, or cuteness. Dunham's short films provide commentary on social expectations, explore sexuality and friendship, and often make the viewer uncomfortable. They did find some popularity on the Oberlin campus, as well as a wider audience later in Dunham's career. In 2010, she included a few of them as extras on the DVD for *Tiny Furniture*. Most of them can still be found on YouTube.

to host the Art Awards at the Guggenheim Museum. Following the awards, the institution put their support behind the second season of *Delusional Downtown Divas*, upping the production value with lighting and sound. About the relevance of the project, Dunham said in an interview, "Now you have people who are like, Yeah, I'm going to be in a band, but if that doesn't work out, I'm probably going to make my living as a painter." She continued, "There's this illusion all of a sudden that it's this financially viable industry to enter into, whereas it used to be that if you decided to be an artist, you were basically deciding to live in an attic and get TB and die."[3] If her goal was to illuminate and roll her eyes at the ideal of the celebrity artist, she may have gotten it just about right. Though the series ended after two seasons, 2009 would bring an even bigger breakthrough for Dunham, on a much bigger screen.

Creative Nonfiction

Dunham's next project would be her long-awaited departure from the low-budget web series. This time, she moved into low-budget mid-length film territory. At just twenty-two years old, Dunham wrote, directed, and starred in her first feature film. This time, the main character didn't share her first name. However, there were still clear parallels between Dunham herself and the story she wove about Ella, a liberal arts student dealing with a disappointing, nonstarting romance and writing a screenplay about a disappointing, nonstarting romance.

She would later discuss the many ways in which *Creative Nonfiction*, and its movie-within-a-movie, closely mirrored her own liberal arts experience, her own lackluster romances, and even her own creative nonfiction classes. The film was shot over the course of one semester at Oberlin College. Talking to *Filmmaker* magazine, Dunham said, "I think I just decided to be in it because I couldn't think of anybody else. My big worry for the audience was: how are people going to feel about watching this annoying, confused girl move around for an hour."[4] In a move away from the **satirical** silliness of *Delusional Downtown Divas* and the short, punch-packing nature of *Tight Shots,* Dunham's longer film required the camera to be trained on her for a full sixty minutes. This next step would ask much of her as an actor, demanding that she find comfort on both sides of the camera and sink into more vulnerability than in past projects.

Familiar hand-held, shaky cameras, some improvised (performed without preparation or a script) dialogue, and a low budget all combined to create a rudimentary, clearly student-shot film. The budget started at $10,000 but grew to about $25,000 as filming went on. "Raw" and "naïve" have been used to describe the film that, one must remember, was a *student* project. It was shot in just four weeks, with six months of postproduction.

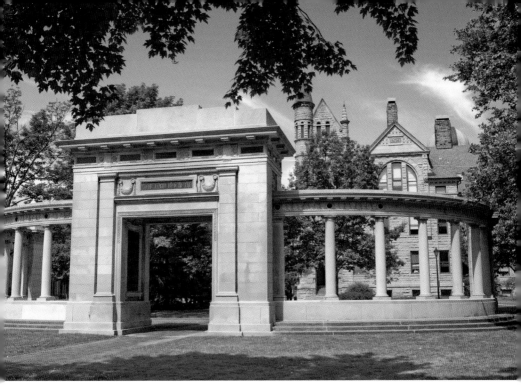
Oberlin College is a private liberal arts college in Oberlin, Ohio.

Again, some of Dunham's favorite themes reemerge here: failed attempts at relationships, vulnerability, and bodies, among other things. The main relationship in the film, between Ella and Chris, is distinguished by Ella's strong desire for a more developed relationship and Chris's lack of desire.

When discussing the real-life experiences she has had that mirror Ella's experience, Dunham has said, "I can't have this issue anymore, I already made a movie about this!"[5] The "issue," at hand seems to be the challenge of taking a friendship into "relationship" territory. Dunham has written and spoken extensively about this challenge and about how confusing it can be to sort through desires and expectations.

Creative Nonfiction was, at its best, a vehicle for Dunham to process and express her frustrations while at Oberlin. In the film, Ella has disappointing social encounters again and again, not only with potential partners, but with female friends, teachers, and classmates. One of the most comical parts of the movie (which shifts swiftly between comedy and drama throughout its sixty-minute run) is a scene in which Ella participates in a **workshop**-style writing class. In a workshop, students read each other's creative work and then openly comment on its merits and problems. This process not only helps the writer improve his or her piece of work, but it offers valuable, though sometimes hard to take, feedback about the writer's work and process in general.

On-screen, Dunham **lampoons** the workshop, making fun of the classic undergraduate workshop experience, while at the same time poking fun at Ella's own screenplay. This type of humor—one that takes itself seriously while also providing comedic commentary and rolling its eyes at the whole endeavor—would become a hallmark of Dunham's later work in *Tiny Furniture* and, eventually, in *Girls*. Dunham knows the world is all-too ready to make fun of her, her art, her body, and more. So she beats the world to the punch by making fun of herself.

Dunham has presented at multiple South by Southwest festivals over the years.

Creative Nonfiction exploded onto the stage at South by Southwest (SXSW), an annual festival of film, media, music, and more, that occurs in Austin, Texas. Each year, the gathering brings together tens of thousands of people for live music, speakers, and screenings. The 2009 edition of the festival featured *Creative Nonfiction* as part of its "Emerging Visions" category. The year before, Dunham applied with a **rough cut**—an unfinished version of the movie with minimal editing. SXSW rejected that version of the film. But the next year, she sent in a finalized version, and it was chosen. Dunham received the call while she was babysitting, which was her main source of income at the time. She later described receiving the call: "I was almost hyperventilating … The little boy I was babysitting was like, 'What's wrong,' and I was like, 'Nothing. Nothing!' Then he stabbed me with a pencil."[6]

For Dunham, the satisfaction of making it into the festival after being rejected was a substantial one. Throughout her life, she has taken great pleasure in bouncing back from rejection, including transferring to Oberlin College after being rejected the year before. She has found a way to trust that rejection isn't an outright dismissal of herself or her projects, but simply a sign that it was not quite the right time. Often, the right time might be right around the corner.

Many filmmakers come to SXSW in the hopes of selling their movie to a distributor, who will get it into movie theaters, onto DVD, or otherwise into the homes of people across the country. Dunham, though, didn't attend the festival with that expectation. At just sixty minutes, her film wasn't feature-length. She wrote it over Oberlin's winter term, a period of weeks in which students are encouraged to focus on independent creative projects. The first draft, finished over January 2006, was just a project for credit. But it took on a life of its own, growing in length, depth, and sophistication.

Critics have praised Dunham's writing, her ability to paint realistic scenes, and her in-your-face approach to awkward, messy subjects. She doesn't shy away from nudity or depicting relationships based on her real-life experiences. That's why, over ten years later, people are still watching her early work, discussing it, and writing about it. These first successes helped to set the stage for her later films and shows, both by letting the world know who she is and why she's here, and by giving Dunham the experience and skills she would need in order to produce better and better work.

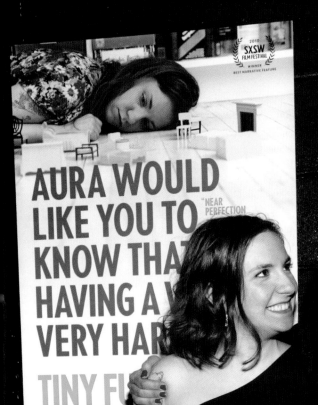

CHAPTER THREE

Entry into the Public Eye

Usually, a writer-director-actor wouldn't be happy with a *New Yorker* article that refers to her projects and, in many ways, herself, as "unwatchable." But Lena Dunham isn't your usual writer-director-actor, and the *New Yorker*, in 2012, didn't declare her film *Tiny Furniture* to be totally horrendous. In an article titled "Lena Dunham: Unwatchable in the Best Way," Lorrie Moore uses words like "depressing," "degrading," and "preciously interesting," but also hints at the thrilling nature of it all, the "TMI," or too much information, that the audience is often left with during Dunham's films and shows.[1] If one is eventually thrust

Lena had her mom's support both on- and offscreen during filming for *Tiny Furniture*.

into the public eye, it may as well be in all of one's honest, awkward, and uncomfortable glory, according to Dunham's perspective. If that makes her movies unwatchable, well, Dunham doesn't seem to have a problem with that. The audience's comfort and even, at times, enjoyment, are not her main priorities.

Tiny Furniture

With *Tiny Furniture*, Dunham produced her first major breakout hit. Released in 2010 at South by Southwest, the movie garnered attention from major publications and critics, earning Dunham credit for perfecting her craft and voice over the years, building into better and better things. This film, perhaps more so than any of her prior work, is somewhat **autobiographical**, or written about her own life. In fact, it draws so much from her own life that, once one is familiar with Dunham's own story, it is difficult to parse out just where her life and the plot of the movie diverge. While *Delusional Downtown Divas* drew from her art-world upbringing, and *Creative Nonfiction* dwelled on her experiences as a college student, *Tiny Furniture* took it a step further.

The film was inspired, both in name and in content, by Dunham's mother, Laurie Simmons. Simmons began her photography career in the late 1970s and has long specialized in **domestic** scenes—images depicting kitchens, living rooms, bedrooms, and chairs. Her 1978 series *Early Color Interiors* was just that: color

In *Tiny Furniture*, Dunham's character finds work as a part-time waitress and falls for one of her coworkers.

photographs of interiors—inside rooms. A 1998 project called *House/Castle* featured carefully lit shots of exteriors. These scenes, however, were not staged in life-size houses. Simmons focused her art specifically on *tiny* furniture, working in miniature, using the scenes to subvert understanding of feminine ideals and the woman's role in the home. Dunham spent her childhood immersed in this art, watching her mother choose sets, place furniture with care, and take photographs. At twenty-two, she decided to let her art imitate her life, casting Simmons, as well as Grace Dunham, Lena's sister, in *Tiny Furniture*. Simmons played an exaggerated, but not wholly inaccurate, version of herself. The character, Siri, was noticeably crabby and not incredibly likable. Her artwork is featured heavily in the film, which includes several minutes of Siri staging her tiny furniture for photographs.

Simmons has commented on the experience of essentially playing her daughter's mother in a movie written and directed by her daughter. In a 2016 interview, she said, "I find Siri to be an excruciating character. I give a lot of credit to my daughter to get me to go to that place. People who saw the film assume that's who I am. I do feel sort of embarrassed. I don't know how I did that."[2] For Dunham, the film was both autobiographical and a piece of art. She played the lead character, Aura, and her sister, Grace, played Aura's younger sister. In fact, the movie was filmed in the family's own Tribeca loft! Though partially comedic, it does spend time exploring the complicated nature of mother-daughter relationships, especially when both the mother and daughter identify as artists. Siri is, at times, both a person to whom Aura turns for support and someone she grates against. In one scene, they scream at each other, and Aura breaks down in tears, shoving piles of mail and paperwork off her mother's workspace before stomping out of the room in the fashion of a four-year-old who has been denied a snack.

Tiny Furniture follows Aura's attempts, after college graduation, to find her own unique path and make a life for herself, all while living in her parents' home and failing, again and again, to fully "launch" her life. The viewer gets an inside look at the parties, jobs, and relationships she experiences immediately after graduation. In the opening scene, she moves back into her mother's all-white loft, hauling her bags and pet hamster across the threshold, and essentially placing herself right back into childhood. She takes up, again, her old bedroom, fighting her younger sister for space and attention. We follow Aura to her first part-time job as a restaurant hostess, her forays into dating, and moments of existential crisis. She tries to chat with the child she's babysitting—he says "N.O." She asks her mother if she can sleep in her bed, and her mother says "No." She can't sleep there unless expressly invited. Aura asks her sister to share with her some personal details about her dating life. Again, the answer is "No."

Aura continues to receive negative answers throughout the months covered in the film. Men reject her, she fights with her mother and sister, she quits her job. But the moments of the movie that are most arresting, and perhaps most true, are the scenes in which Aura is given what she wants—be it a man, a friend, a situation—and realizes that her expectations do not actually line up with reality at all. At its heart, the film is about being stuck and about feeling disappointed. It is about the failure of relationships, be they familial or otherwise. As Dunham's first feature-length film, it was naturally about her and her life, and what audiences could expect from her work going forward.

The response to *Tiny Furniture* was mixed but generally favorable. Some critics have called it "revolutionary," citing its mumblecore roots, funny dialogue, and realistic portrayals of complicated, messy relationships. Others have declared the movie is not relatable, a criticism that would follow Dunham into her other projects, most notably *Girls*. With the Tribeca loft, successful artist mother, and apparent lack of need for a job or direction, the scene in *Tiny Furniture* isn't a slice-of-life film for the majority of Americans. It does retain a high rating on Rotten Tomatoes, a popular movie review website, and the movie remains available for streaming online, seven years after its first release.

Gender, Race, and Class in *Tiny Furniture*

Other critiques of the film focus primarily on Dunham's approach to gender. Today, one popular way of categorizing and critiquing a film is by putting it to the test—the **Bechdel test**, to be exact. To "pass" the Bechdel test, a movie must meet three criteria. It must have at least two named female characters, those characters must talk to each other, and those characters must talk about something other than a man. Many, many feature films do not pass this test. In fact, most films shown in United States theaters do not pass this test. In *Tiny Furniture,* there are two male characters, and those characters are central components of the plot, but the story also revolves around the relationships between female characters. The mother-daughter relationship is central. In many scenes, Aura reads from her mother's old diaries from her time as

The cast of *Tiny Furniture* included family, friends, and actors who would later work on some of Dunham's other projects.

a twenty-something, and most of their arguments revolve around Aura's desire to sleep next to her mother in bed, like a small child might. Dunham's real-life sister, Grace, plays her on-screen sister, Nadine, who is both years younger and seemingly more mature than Aura. During one of the movie's emotional **apexes**, Nadine and Aura devolve into a screaming match, cutting each other down in front of their respective friends—Nadine's, a room full of teenagers, and Aura's, her sole confidante and wayward friend, Charlotte. Unlike so many films throughout history and today, *Tiny Furniture* puts complicated female relationships front and center and emphasizes the ways in which they do not revolve around men. Interestingly, Aura's interactions with men in the film are generally kept separate, and often secret, and they are threaded through with a negativity that doesn't come from other women. It comes from them, and from inside herself.

Both in the middle of scenes with male characters and in scenes featuring just herself or other women, Dunham does make a point to draw the viewer's attention to one thing that her critics and fans have long sparred over—her body. In fact, Dunham's body—which is curvy, pale, and delightfully "average"—is featured over and over again. Whether she's walking around her kitchen in a t-shirt and underwear, getting ready to go out for the evening, or changing into pajamas for the night, Dunham lets the audience get a realistic view of those moments when a person is vulnerable, undressed, and unadorned. For many viewers, especially young women, Dunham's conscious choice to put her body on display, though it is not *conventionally* attractive and does not conform to society's popular understanding of "sexy," is a powerful one. It sends the message that all bodies are beautiful, valid, and worthy of being on-screen. For others, her body is something to comment on, laugh at, and ridicule.

After receiving attention for *Creative Nonfiction* and *Tiny Furniture*, Dunham's earlier works began to get more hits on YouTube, as people became interested in the writer-director. When she went back to look at the comments on films like *The Fountain*, she found herself scrolling through paragraphs full of hate. "There were just pages of YouTube comments about how fat I was, or how not fat I was, or saying, 'That's not a fat girl—go to Detroit and see a *real* fat girl.'"[3] Tiring of the comments, Dunham ended up taking *The Fountain* off the internet, though a clip from the video is still featured in *Tiny Furniture*. In it, Dunham is so young, and so unapologetically herself, standing in a fountain in the middle of the Oberlin campus in minimal clothing, that it is difficult to imagine the hate that is hurled at her, and her appearance, through the internet. But as long as she's been making shows and films, people have been talking about Dunham's body. Over and over again in the reviews of *Tiny Furniture*, critics brought her body to the forefront of the discussion, even if they enjoyed the movie and had positive comments about Dunham's choices in regard to clothing and nudity. Unfortunately, no matter how hard she might try, it is difficult for a female writer-director to be taken seriously, or to be seen for anything other than her physical presence. This issue would continue to follow Dunham throughout her professional life.

Critics have also noted, along with the political and social commentary that comes with the choice to display an "imperfect" body, that Dunham's movies provide further commentary on both class and race. To some extent in *Creative Nonfiction*, and to a greater degree in *Tiny Furniture*, it is clear that Dunham, and her characters, are inhabiting and representing a particular

Once she entered the public eye, Dunham was overwhelmed with requests for interviews.

level of **affluence**. From the loft in Manhattan to the private college tuition that seems to come without student loans, Dunham's family isn't exactly living a middle-class lifestyle. Dunham's character, Aura, is mildly interested in work, but she feels no pressure whatsoever to get (or keep) a job. When she eats her family's food, drinks her mother's wine, or otherwise spends money, there seem to be no tangible consequences. Though not clearly excessive, the film (and most of Dunham's later work) takes for granted this affluent lifestyle. At times, she seems to joke about it. But many writers have critiqued her lack of clear commentary, suggesting loudly that Dunham needs to take a hard look at her work and see if she can produce something more relatable. She was, however, raised within that world of wealth and privilege (special rights or advantages granted to a specific person or group of people), and it is likely for this reason that she chooses to write about characters with wealth and privilege—it's simply what she knows best.

That privilege reveals itself in another way in *Tiny Furniture* and throughout Dunham's entire body of work—through her engagement, or lack of engagement, with race. It is important to note that nearly all of the characters in the film are white, and nearly all of the characters in her future projects would be white. In *Tiny Furniture*, we see glimpses of nonwhite people, but they are limited to busboys and cooks at the restaurant where Aura works for a short time. Critics have had much to say on this subject, some calling Dunham out for not trying harder to show true diversity on-screen, especially as a woman, **feminist**, and young person who has the power to draw audiences and respect through her art. Others, such as *n+1* writer Elizabeth Gumport, insist that Dunham must simply continue to be true to her own lived experience, which, for better or worse, has been primarily a world of affluent, white privilege. Gumport writes of the critics, "There's no reason she should be made to pay for the fact that some people live in Park Slope. We ought instead to be inspired by Dunham's allegiance to her own experience—to having it, to recording it."[4] The jury is still

In 2011, Dunham won the Best First Screenplay award for *Tiny Furniture* during the Film Independent Spirit Awards in California.

out on how, or if, Dunham will open up her writing to include a more diverse pool of characters and experiences. For now, film critic Glenn Kenny may have hit the nail on the head when he tweeted, "I think *Tiny Furniture* is good, but it does represent the Cinema of Unexamined Privilege, let's face it."[5]

Recognition and Next Steps

According to Dunham, *Tiny Furniture* only cost about $65,000 to make. No doubt, this number was kept low thanks to the many actors who were Dunham's own family members and friends, as well as the choice to use her family's loft and the New York City street as the main set of the film. After premiering at South by Southwest in March 2010, the movie was shown at several other festivals, including the Denver International, Oslo International, Los Angeles, and Birds Eye View Film Festivals, among others. It was screened at festivals across the United States and Europe, making nearly $400,000 at the box office and picking up several awards as it went along. At SXSW, it won the Narrative Feature Award and the Chicken and Egg Emergent Narrative Woman Director Award. She was nominated for Breakthrough Director at the Gotham Awards, and her cast was nominated there for Best Ensemble Performance. At the Film Independent Spirit Awards in 2011, Dunham won the award for Best First Screenplay. All of this recognition not only served to build up Dunham's popularity as a writer and director, but it also added real "evidence" to the idea that Dunham was in the right place professionally, doing exactly what she should be.

In 2012, *Tiny Furniture* was released on DVD. The release was managed by the Criterion Collection, Inc., which is a prestigious home video distribution company known for releasing classic and important films. With all of the success from *Tiny Furniture*, one could easily picture Dunham writing and directing, and even acting in, another feature-length film, even one that might make it to wide distribution across theaters. Instead of jumping

Lena Dunham and Nora Ephron

When critics and writers share their commentary on *Tiny Furniture,* just like any other film, they often like to share their ideas about what other films and directors they think inspired Dunham to write her movie. Was she inspired by other mumblecore writers? With her exploration of New York City and attention to dialogue, was she paying homage to Woody Allen? It's hard to say what has propelled Dunham to make any of her films and shows, but she has spoken to this herself in interviews and essays. According to Dunham, she was influenced heavily by Nora Ephron, the late writer, screenwriter, producer, and director who is best known for her romantic comedies. *Sleepless in Seattle, When Harry Met Sally*, and *Julie & Julia* are some of her most popular films. Dunham, of course, was a huge fan of her autobiographical work. In a piece for the *New Yorker*, Dunham wrote, *"This Is My Life* [which

to a new script, Dunham rode the wave of her movie, getting it in front of as many viewers as possible, until she found just the audience she was looking for—Judd Apatow, notable writer, director, producer, and comedian. Apatow, upon seeing the movie, immediately emailed Dunham a message full of praise. Speaking to the *New Yorker*, Apatow remembered, "About twenty minutes in, I

Ephron wrote] is the movie that made me want to make movies."[6]

After receiving an email from Ephron in 2011 that said she liked Dunham's film, Dunham embarked on a beautiful, if short, friendship with the director, whom she had always looked up to and aspired to emulate. Dunham refers to Ephron's advice as "unparalleled." They kept in close contact, talking on the phone, emailing, and meeting up in person. A conversation between the two is featured on the *Tiny Furniture* DVD. In the summer of 2012, Ephron passed away from pneumonia due to complications from leukemia, which she was diagnosed with in 2006. Dunham's final word on her dear friend, in the *New Yorker*, was this: "The opportunity to be friends with Nora in the last year of her life informs the entirety of mine. I am so grateful."[7]

turned to my wife and I said, 'Am I crazy, or is this kind of unbelievably great?'"[8] Apatow and Dunham would go on to collaborate on what is arguably Dunham's main contribution to film and television—at least so far.

CHAPTER FOUR

Lena Dunham's Contributions and Success

When moviemaker Judd Apatow watched Lena Dunham's *Tiny Furniture* for the first time, he felt an instant connection to the characters, the script, and the writer-director behind the project. He immediately emailed Dunham to ask for a meeting. Dunham, of course, was delighted to hear from

In 2012, Dunham would debut her biggest success so far: *Girls*.

him, as she was already familiar with Apatow's work, especially his short-lived but insanely popular television show *Freaks and Geeks*, as well as "bro humor" movies such as *Knocked Up* and *The 40-Year-Old Virgin*. The two talked on the phone and over email, pitching ideas back and forth, searching for one with potential for collaboration and, ultimately, television success. When they met face-to-face, any anxieties dissipated. They were meant to work together.

Though Dunham's projects tend to center on and focus their energies around the lives of women, she wasn't entirely put off by Apatow's film history. In fact, she related to the "outsider" experiences that many of Apatow's characters had, especially those in *Freaks and Geeks*. From their very first meeting, the two began to foster a deeply collaborative environment between themselves, and they enjoyed a nearly seamless transition from friends to professional partners. Dunham described the process to the *New York Times*: "Judd is also deeply collaborative in a way I wasn't when we started. I was raised by artists who went into their studios alone and came out with their work. That was the creative process. So Judd and Jenni [Konner] had to introduce me to collaboration."[1] Despite these hiccups in the beginning, the two meshed well together, and they eventually produced the pilot for what would become an award-winning, critically acclaimed HBO show—*Girls*.

Girls, a thirty-minute-per-episode comedy about four friends living out their post-college lives in Brooklyn,

Hannah, Marnie, Jessa, and Shoshanna were four characters with very unique personalities and styles.

New York, premiered in April 2012. Dunham, who wrote and produced the show, also played the main character, Hannah Horvath. Hannah is an aspiring writer living in Brooklyn, two years after graduating from Oberlin College (Dunham's alma mater). In the pilot episode, Hannah's parents sit her down and, over dinner, inform her that they will no longer be supporting her financially. She will have to find a job and make her own way in the world. The six seasons that follow the pilot episode follow Hannah and her social circle as they make their way, for better or worse, through their twenties.

Any young woman who watches *Girls* on a regular basis has probably had the following question asked of her: "Are you Hannah, Marnie, Jessa, or Shoshanna?" Though women are far too unique and complex to be dropped easily into one of four categories, many viewers still enjoy matching themselves up with one of the four strong personalities in the show. The women have their own quirks, histories, and talents.

Marnie Marie Michaels is Hannah's responsible New York City roommate and best friend from Oberlin College. Throughout the show, she moves from art gallery assistant to aspiring musician. Jessa Johansson recently returned to New York after living abroad. Jessa is Hannah's most unpredictable and irresponsible friend. She struggles with drug addiction and relationship challenges across all six seasons. Shoshanna Shapiro is an innocent and naïve college student. Shoshanna navigates the city with the help of her friends and struggles, all along, to find the right career path.

Portions of the characters, as well as chunks of their storylines, were inspired by Dunham's own life experiences. She did graduate from Oberlin, and she did, for years, struggle to find her direction, purpose, and financial stability following college graduation. Like the characters in the series, Dunham has experienced a number of disappointing, unfulfilling relationships, and her familial relationships, while close-knit, have had their share of tension, especially due to the success and stability of her parents. The characters in the show represent a specific wealthy class of the young, white, well-educated, straight millennial population (born between the early 1980s and 2004), which Dunham has said she chose deliberately and carefully. Growing up, Dunham was a huge fan of the HBO show *Sex and the City*, but she did not see her own *particular* type of New York City woman represented on television, and she felt this was a glaring void. Her vision for the show may be best expressed in the following sentences, a portion of Dunham's original pitch for the show:

> *Products of the recession, these girls are overeducated and underemployed, sure that they're too smart for their positions as assistants, nannies, and waitresses but not necessarily motivated enough to prove it (or even do their jobs well enough to advance) ...*

They have varying degrees of ambition, but have been raised to achieve. They know they want to be successful long before they know what they want to be successful at.

They're the last children of baby boomers, and the first generation to have moms who know how to text message ...

Grad school is their fall-back plan.

They are the Facebook generation, and ironically enough they are isolated by all the connectivity available to them ...

They're beautiful and maddening. They're self-aware and self-obsessed. They're your girlfriends and daughters and sisters and employees. They're my friends and I've never seen them on TV. [2]

Because she wasn't seeing these types of women on television, Dunham decided to write them herself and act them herself. HBO gave Dunham and her team an extreme amount of freedom to write and produce the show exactly as they saw fit. Working with Apatow and Konner, Dunham was able to rein in her tell-all, show-all personality a little bit, where necessary, in order to make *Girls* the best show it could be. Working together, the dream team produced six seasons full of episodes that were uniquely funny, emotionally arresting, painfully realistic (for some), and simply interesting enough that viewers came back to watch again and again.

Initial Reception

Throughout its run, *Girls* received criticism for portraying a rather narrow view of the New York City borough,

Brooklyn, where the series is set, and for lacking diversity in general. Dunham, with her outspoken, progressive voice, was needled by the critics who pushed her to make the show more inclusive. In the pilot episode, Hannah Horvath describes herself, jokingly, as the "voice of her generation," and many viewers took that statement to mean that Dunham purports herself to be that same voice. The bar, then, was raised higher. If the show was going to speak for a generation, it had to speak for the whole generation—including people of color, queer individuals, and those on all points of the economic scale. This was a major pressure point for viewers throughout the run of the series, though Dunham addressed some situations as they came up. In response to the initial public outcry, for example, Dunham made the following statement:

I wrote the first season primarily by myself, and I co-wrote a few episodes. But I am a half-Jew, half-WASP, and I wrote two Jews and two WASPs. Something I wanted to avoid was tokenism in casting. If I had one of the four girls, if, for example, she was African American, I feel like— not that the experience of an African American girl and a white girl are drastically different, but there has to be specificity to that experience [that] I wasn't able to speak to. I really wrote the show from a gut-level place, and each character was a piece of me or based on someone close to me. And only later did I realize that it was four white girls. As much as I can say it was an accident, it was only later as the criticism came out, I thought, "I hear this and I want to respond to it." And this is a hard issue to speak to because all I want to do is sound sensitive and not say anything that will horrify anyone or make them feel more isolated, but I did write something that was super-specific to my experience, and I always want to avoid rendering an experience I can't speak to accurately.[3]

For many, the lack of diversity was off-putting at best. Dunham tried to improve the character diversity somewhat, but the show's four main characters remained themselves, and their circle of friends and boyfriends was not dissimilar. Other viewers connected readily and deeply with the show—laughing at all the jokes, understanding the characters' life situations, and, ultimately, wanting to see more. The unpaid internships, social anxiety, and confessional feel of the show sits squarely inside the life experience of many viewers. For those who "get" the show, they really "get it," and they *love* it.

Honest and Personal

One of the most talked-about aspects of *Girls* is also one of the most visual—Dunham's body. Throughout her career, Dunham has deliberately written her body into countless scenes and put it into so many awkward,

Dunham not only acted in *Girls*, but she also wrote and directed the episodes.

uncomfortable positions that one can hardly keep track! She films herself in intimate scenes, at the doctor's office, in the bathtub, everywhere. Nudity on television is not rare, but nudity that isn't airbrushed, careful, and perfect is hard to find. Dunham films herself with broken-out skin. She films her body when it's bloated, with all of its natural shapes and shadows. She films at unflattering angles, with lots of uncomfortable dialogue sprinkled in for good measure. Some of the scenes are cringe-worthy, and nearly all of them are remarkably realistic.

Throughout the run of the series, Dunham was sure to prioritize that realism and honesty, though that tendency was often criticized. Dunham is a "sharer," and she has been from childhood. In *Girls*, not only does she share herself and her own life, but the viewer is also given a very up-close-and-personal look at the lives of the characters she has created. We see the messes they make of their lives, and we see their heartbreak and poor decisions. The viewer is often made to feel annoyed by the characters, or even disgusted. Dunham's choice to share her personal experiences through film and television is a calculated one. Her best friend, creative partner, and show runner, Jenni Konner, says of Dunham, "Something happens to Lena the night before, she literally comes in the next day and pitches it."[4] Some of the lines in *Tiny Furniture*, especially those uttered by the male characters, were taken straight from Dunham's experiences, from the mouths of ex-boyfriends and friends. In *Girls*, while the lines aren't all quotations, many of the scenes hint at, or even deeply engage with, real moments from Dunham's own life. Here, she shares her feelings about the criticism that has been lobbed at her for telling her stories:

> *You know, I think the term over sharing is so complicated because I do think it's really gendered. I think that when men ... share their experiences, it's bravery, and [when] women share their experiences ... people are like TMI. Too much information has always been my least favorite phrase because what exactly constitutes too much information? It seems like it has a lot to do with who is giving you the information. And I feel as though there's some sense that society trivializes female experiences. And so when you share them, they aren't ... considered as vital as their male counterparts. And that's something that I've always roundly rejected.*[5]

That round rejection, which Dunham utilizes over and over in her work—rejection of conventions, rejection of criticism, rejection of fear—helped to propel Dunham and her team forward and kept the show going, despite its detractors, for six seasons. No matter what, the show's resident writer-director-actor-producer has pushed the envelope and stayed true to her own vision and voice. Though *Girls* has concluded its final season, the ripples that have resulted from its impact will last for a long time. The show has clearly influenced the television being produced around and after it, such as shows featuring

The End of an Era

As *Girls* came to its close after six seasons, viewers witnessed a world of changes for each young woman on the show. Dunham's character, Hannah Horvath, made the biggest change of all in the first half of the last season—she became pregnant. Viewers were almost as shocked as Hannah, who went to the doctor to check for an infection and left with the knowledge that she might have a baby. Fans were abuzz with the news, curious to see what Hannah would decide to do about her pregnancy. Dunham weighed in in an interview with *Vanity Fair*: "It's been interesting to have some people be like, 'I can't wait until you get that abortion next week,' and other people were like, 'This is the most exciting thing, when are you having [the baby]?'" She continued, "It brings up interesting debates."[6]

strong female writer-actors like *Inside Amy Schumer*, *The Mindy Project*, and *Broad City*.

Dunham has come far since 2012, when the characters she was writing, with all of their confusion, lack of direction, and lack of experience, mirrored her own life and the lives of her friends. In the final season, Hannah Horvath works with the *New York Times*, Marnie gets married and navigates that relationship, Shoshanna moves in with her former boyfriend, and Jessa dates Hannah's ex-boyfriend. All four stories ultimately shifted far away from where they originally started, and

The pregnancy plotline, an entirely new one for the show, gave audiences the chance to project their own political opinions onto the characters. While critics and fans alike had long aired their political and social grievances with the show, this particular plotline seemed to invite debate and controversy. Writer Anna Silman succinctly captures the issue:

> The pregnancy implicates us as viewers, forcing us to examine our own biases and preconceptions about what it means for a woman like Hannah to choose to become a mother. And just as [the other characters'] reactions say more about them than they do about Hannah, our responses say more about us as viewers than they do about *Girls*. It's a neat trick, for a show that's often seemed encumbered by the baggage that others have piled onto it. Here, *Girls* is doing what it's lately done best and most intelligently: engaging on a meta level with the conversation it inspires.[7]

the friend group began to fray at the edges somewhat. Reflecting on the progress of the show in 2015, at the start of its fourth season, Dunham told *Elle* magazine, "I used to have this thought where we'd have four perfect seasons and disappear in a burst of flames, and now I'm like we should do this until we are sixty, and then all the characters should have grandchildren and then we should follow them."[8] While she may not have been ready to leave Hannah, Marnie, Shoshanna, and Jessa behind, she is always ready to tackle other projects and adventures.

CHAPTER FIVE

Activism

When *Girls* was picked up by HBO in 2012, Lena Dunham was only twenty-five years old. Technically an adult, she was still deep in the prolonged adolescence that often accompanies those of the millennial generation into their twenties. Still, she had to quickly learn how to combine her roles as writer, director, and actor, alongside newfound celebrity. She had to grow up fast and be her own boss, and suddenly, she was also the boss of others. She was being watched, quite literally, by paparazzi and by young people across the country. Women began to look to her for guidance and inspiration; some male viewers became fans, while others turned into trolls on the internet, which are people who start arguments and upset people by posting inflammatory content. The main goal of

Leading up to the 2016 presidential election, Dunham was a very vocal supporter of Hillary Clinton.

a person who is "trolling" is to provoke an emotional response. These trolls, as well as true fans, turned to Dunham both on- and offscreen, listening to her every word in interviews and watching closely to see where her passions would lie when it came to life outside the script.

Lena Dunham's Influence

In the pilot episode (the standalone, and often first, episode of a series used to sell it to a network or channel) of *Girls*, Dunham's character, Hannah Horvath, famously utters this line to her parents: "I don't want to freak you out, but I think that I may be the voice of my generation. Or at least, *a* voice of *a* generation." While endless jokes have been made and many have rolled their eyes at Hannah's (and Dunham's, presumably) **insinuation** that one or both of them might speak for their generation, it is worth noting that, in many ways, Dunham does just that. Her hit television show and seemingly endless media commentary give her the opportunity to speak on almost any platform she chooses. From gender expectations to LGBTQ issues, from politics to body positivity, Dunham has spoken up and spoken out on a range of subjects. In 2014, *Time* added her to its list of the "100 Most Influential People." As long as magazines keep publishing interviews and her quotes keep appearing in the headlines, Dunham will be, at least, *a* voice of *a* generation.

In an interview with *Elle* magazine writer Jessica Pressler, Dunham explained:

I realized early on that I was not going to be able to have a comfortable relationship with celebrity if I didn't feel like I was using it to talk about things that were important to me. It was always going to make me feel gross, for lack of a better word. I was like, "Oh, this attention is something I'm going to figure out how to use in a way that feels productive, healthy, and smart. And not just like as an excuse to collect handbags." Although, ... I love handbags.[1]

Within her newfound celebrity from the success of *Girls*, it has become important to Dunham to speak openly about her opinions on political and social issues. She was involved in social and political movements from a young age thanks to guidance from her mother. Laurie Simmons, who was part of the Women's Action Coalition, took her daughters to protests in New York City. Simmons has described her thought process as a young mom: "I'm just going to take them along, let them witness this other part of my life that I'm really passionate about."[2] For Lena and Grace, that meant attending rallies and actions of many kinds, often holding signs in their strollers and soaking in the atmosphere of passionate, political people making strong statements about their communities, their country, and their lives. This sense of political activism, so strongly planted in childhood, lay dormant inside Dunham during her college years. She avoided activism and even avoided voting until she was twenty-two years old! However,

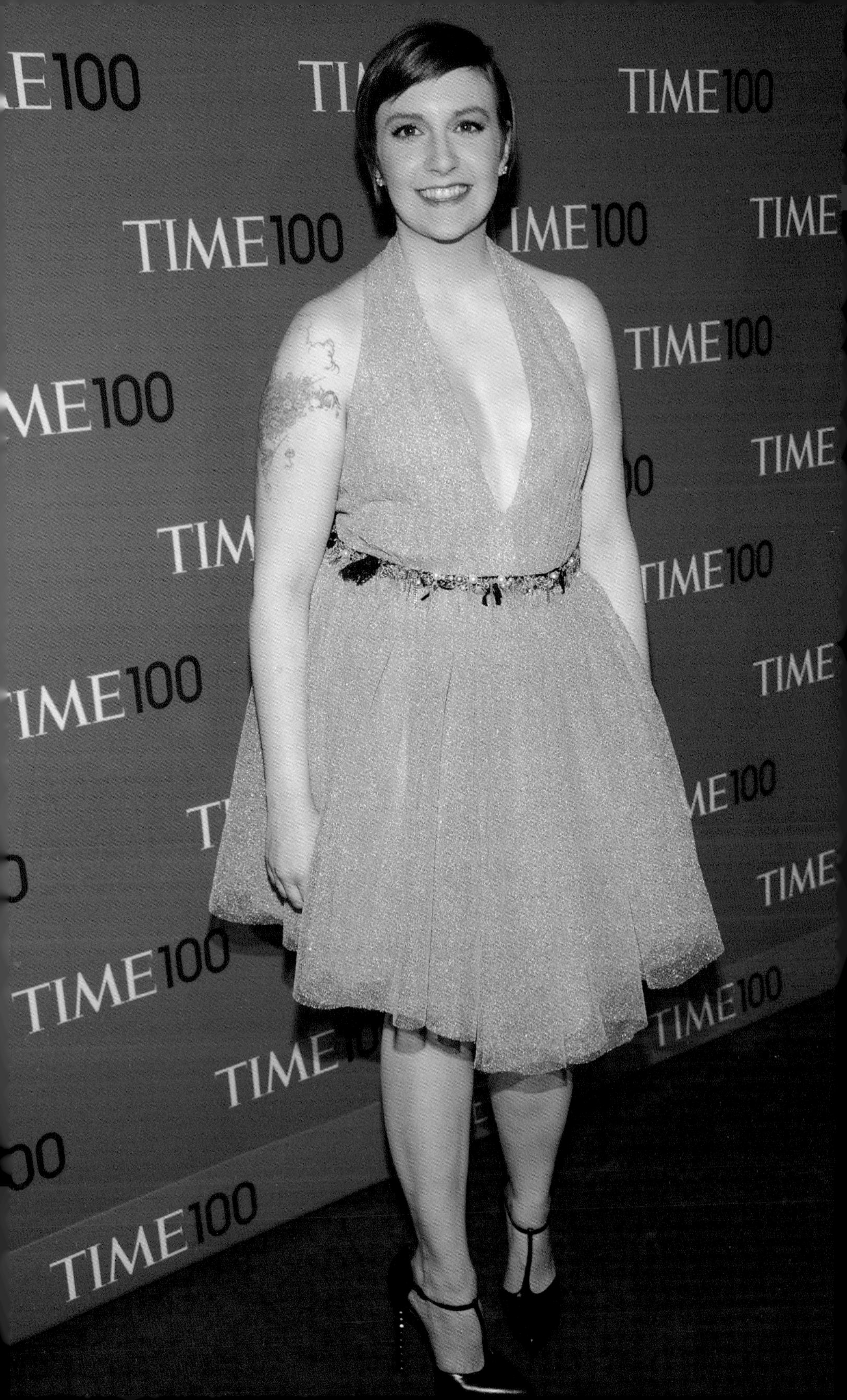
TIME100

after *Girls* premiered, Dunham felt compelled to become active in politics again. In one interview, she described the thought she had: "I have two choices: either to hide from this and Instagram pictures of my favorite lipstick, or to embrace it."[3] For now, it seems, she has embraced it, speaking out on everything from her favored political candidate to her thoughts on Planned Parenthood, immigrant rights, and much more.

On International Women's Day in 2017, Dunham posted an open letter online, writing about the inspiration behind her activism: her grandmother and namesake, Lena, who traveled to Brooklyn from Russia. In the letter, Dunham compared her own teenage interests—shopping, skipping Hebrew school, and getting her belly button pierced—to the immense challenges her grandmother faced as a young immigrant and mother. She wrote of her dedication to channeling her grandmother, not just in small ways, but "in big ways, too, like bearing life's trials and tribulations— physical and emotional—with as much elegance as I can muster. By taking action against silent injustice. By trying my darnedest to feed those I love—if not with my own hands then with love, patience, compassion, and takeout."[4] Though this was one of the first times Dunham shared stories about the inspirational woman compelling her to take a stand, it was not the first time

Dunham shows off her edgy style on the *Time* 100 red carpet.

she had spoken out. In fact, her tenure with political movements got started over five years earlier, when Barack Obama was running for reelection.

Politics

In 2012, just as *Girls* got going, the Obama campaign asked Dunham to make a video encouraging first-time voters to register and vote. The video was outwardly feminist and edgy, causing conservatives to call out the clip as "astoundingly tasteless."[5] According to Dunham, the video didn't seem controversial at all, and the blowback came as an unwelcome surprise. But she didn't let that stop her from making her voice heard in the national political arena. Four years later, when Hillary Clinton entered the race for the presidency, Dunham was there alongside her, making speeches at primary events, writing persuasive pieces online, and even making new videos promoting the candidate (with her usual mix of outrageous honesty and comedy). She felt strongly that Clinton should and would be the winner in November 2016; after spending eighteen months working with Clinton and her supporters, and especially after traveling to the swing states in the last few weeks, Dunham was sure the Democratic Party could pull off a win. She was ready to celebrate. She was already planning how she would describe the victory to her future children.

In an open letter written after Election Day, Dunham described the day after the election as "a day of mourning."[6] She described the deep pain of losing, especially after such a passionate, long, important fight. She described, in great detail, the hopelessness of that day, and of the days after. Then she called on every American to find, somewhere inside, a little bit of hope. She wrote:

> *So no, the work isn't done. It is only beginning. We will stun ourselves with what we are capable of. We will laugh with surprise like kids who finally threw a punch back at the schoolyard bully. We will watch our friends in awe as they step forward and demand more, as they recognize and wield their politicized identities. We will not be governed by fear. We will show our children a different way. We will go home like shooting stars.*[7]

Supporting Asghar Farhadi

In her letter, Dunham also wrote that we must now "use the tools we have to speak for ourselves, but moreover speak for the voiceless, the people who can't demand change for fear of very real and violent losses."[8] Since that day, she has adjusted her priorities accordingly. She is speaking up on even more issues, and on even larger platforms. In so many ways, she is continuing the work that she insists we must keep doing, the work of stepping forward and refusing to be governed by fear. In 2017, Dunham stepped forward against the proposed ban on travelers from specific countries, often referred to as the "Muslim ban." Taking a break from her own work,

Dunham switched gears in February to support Asghar Farhadi, an Iranian director and Oscar winner who was nominated for another Oscar in 2017. Dunham hosted a screening of Farhadi's film *About Elly* and donated the proceeds to the Council for American-Islamic Relations. She was hoping to build community among artists and allies and to raise awareness about the ban and those affected by it. Farhadi ultimately boycotted the Academy Awards ceremony even though the ban was halted. His film *The Salesman* won the Oscar, and Anousheh Ansari, the first Iranian in space, accepted the award on his behalf. The publicity surrounding Dunham's screening allowed many more people to become aware of his work.

Planned Parenthood

In addition to her newly vocal stance on immigration, Dunham has also continued to support Planned Parenthood, an issue about which she has always been passionate. Dunham's mother, Laurie Simmons, often took Lena and Grace to protests in support of reproductive rights when they were children. Simmons also traveled to clinics around New York State in order to escort and protect women from violent protesters. These actions were not lost on her daughter—Lena was watching and learning. In January 2017, she released a powerful animated video in support of Planned Parenthood. Narrated by Jennifer Lawrence, Mindy Kaling, Amy Schumer, Sasheer Zamata, Meryl Streep,

Dunham remains a vocal advocate for Planned Parenthood and women's reproductive rights.

and other strong women, the film celebrated the organization's hundredth birthday and called attention to its long history, as well as the importance of its existence in the future. Additionally, Dunham brought her sister, Grace, along on her recent eleven-city book tour and put her in charge of making awareness and activism a main component of the tour. Grace, a graduate from Brown University, brought representatives from Planned Parenthood to each stop on the tour and arranged for Lena to participate in a Q&A for employees at a health clinic in Texas. Writing workshops and other events were included on the tour, and Dunham wore T-shirts supporting the organization throughout the stops. She even designed her own T-shirt for the Planned Parenthood Education Fund. The pink crew neck includes a drawing of boxing gloves and says "Don't Hang Up the Gloves," encouraging people to continue the fight for access to reproductive health care.

For Dunham, helping to correct misinformation is key to the work needed in order to support women and Planned Parenthood. In an interview with *Time* about the hundredth-anniversary video, she said, "I think the most powerful thing we can do is reject apathy and raise our voices and engage with people who disagree with us and let young women, specifically, know that they do have a say in whether or not their healthcare is taken away from them."[9] That "say" in the conversation is something that Dunham believes is important for all people to have. Throughout her years as an activist, she has stumbled, at times, to protect or empower the voices of others above her own, but she continues to try. In the same conversation with *Time*, she said:

I never have an interest in defining any other woman's feminism for them, but I do think it's very important to remember feminism is a set of political beliefs born out of the idea that women should have certain essential rights, whether it's the right to vote, the right to own property or the right to make decisions about their own bodies.

I also think a big part of feminism is making room for other women to make choices you don't necessarily agree with. I have no problem sitting down with someone who feels that abortion is not something that they would personally be able to go through with. I do think that when you step into the territory of trying to limit and control other women's bodies, to me that's not a feminist act.[10]

Feminism

At times, Dunham has spoken out about her opinions in ways that have offended or upset individuals and even entire groups of people. Her language can be **polarizing**—it can divide people into groups, which is especially unfortunate when she is hoping, above all else, to bring people together in community and conversation. With her celebrity status and platform come responsibility, and she is still working on finding the right words to say in some situations, as well as the right times to stay silent and let others speak.

Dunham says she works to educate herself and absorb new information. However, many find that Dunham's particular brand of feminism—the political, ideological, and social movements that combine to advance rights for women, as well as the belief that women and men should have equal rights and opportunities—doesn't go quite far enough. While Dunham does have the popular children's-book character Eloise (who she refers to as a "little feminist rebel nightmare") tattooed on her body, and while she calls herself a feminist and works to help advance the rights of women, the feminism that resonates with Dunham does not always match up with other definitions and understandings of feminism.[11]

As an outspoken and honest person, Dunham has had many verbal "flubs," especially when it comes to feminist issues. She has been called out for making comments about abortion that caused many people to feel uncomfortable, for which she later apologized. She has also made racially insensitive comments, including in an interview that appeared on her own website and on social media. For many of these comments, Dunham has apologized. For some, she has not. And that's why the conversation around her feminism, her activism, and her privilege is ongoing.

Of course, for a celebrity, dealing with public scrutiny is part of everyday life. When a celebrity takes up political and social causes, hoping to be a powerful voice in turbulent times, that scrutiny becomes even more constant and intense. Hopefully, criticism by women, feminists, people of color, and others will help to refine and recalibrate the words that come out of her mouth and keyboard; otherwise, she may face resistance to her activism for a long, long time.

Bodies

In addition to activism through speeches, videos, merchandise, social media, and open letters, Dunham has also used her television show and movies as a platform for issues that she holds very close to her heart. Though *Girls* has been met with criticism on many fronts, including its narrow visions of class and race, it has also been praised for highlighting something that isn't often given screen time—the bodies of real women.

Since her very first short films were uploaded to YouTube, Dunham has been making a powerful statement about women's bodies, their value, and their role both on-screen and in life. For Dunham, the prevailing messages we receive about women's and girls' bodies through television and movies—that they must be a certain size and shape (namely, small), tanned, toned, petite, tall, and curvy all at once—are damaging and inconsistent with reality. Women's bodies come in millions of different shapes and sizes; every single one is unique. For Dunham, this is something to be celebrated and affirmed. She affirms this fact by putting her own body on display, over and over again, in nearly every show or movie she has made.

In *Girls*, as in her other projects, it is occasionally jarring to see Dunham in minimal clothing, even if her character is simply getting ready for bed or wandering around her own home. Most women are not often put on display in this way, especially in scenarios that are not romantic or sexual. For Dunham, nudity is a part of everyday life, and she wants to highlight that in her work. Ever since the show first aired, people have regularly mocked Dunham for this stance. The internet trolls have come out by the hundreds (perhaps thousands, or more), calling her any number of disparaging names and writing long, gross descriptions of her body on internet message boards. Some say that the nudity on *Girls* is excessive, but Dunham maintains that the nudity remains because people, in real life, are often naked.

Though she will probably always have critics who spend time ranting about her body, many people believe that Dunham's choice to be nearly naked and naked on-screen is one of bravery. By being open about her body, with all of its unique parts and flaws and beauty, she is allowing more women, especially young women, to be comfortable with their own bodies.

She is also opening up the conversation about what it means to be a woman and what it means to be in control of your body. As the writer and director of her projects, it is Dunham who gets to decide what her characters

Dunham has always been true to her style, her body, and her whole self, no matter the occasion.

wear, how much they wear, and how much of the show they spend without their clothes on. Dunham continues to put herself in uncomfortable and often humiliating situations for the sake of her art. In an interview that appeared in the *Guardian*, she said of watching the hateful comments roll in after each new episode of *Girls*, "You know, it gets easier and easier. My fears came true: people called me fat and hideous, and I lived. And now I keep living."[12]

LGBTQ

In addition to writing and advocating for that which she knows personally—womanhood, reproductive freedom, body positivity—Dunham has also worked to advance the rights of LGBTQ individuals, those who identify as lesbian, gay, bisexual, transgender, and/or queer.

Her sister, Grace, came out as queer a few years ago, and since that time, Dunham has been outspoken on issues of LGBTQ rights. In 2014, she received the Horizon Award from the Point Foundation in recognition of her work on behalf of the LGBTQ community. In a speech made while receiving her award, Dunham said the following:

In 2014, Dunham accepted an award from the Point Foundation in recognition of her work on behalf of the LGBTQ community.

Activist and Ally

For Lena Dunham, her family's acceptance of Grace's sexual orientation is the ideal. It is her hope that any and all young people have a positive and affirming family and support system. In addition to involving Grace in the activist side of her book tour, Dunham coproduced a 2016 documentary for HBO, *Suited*, that revolves around queer-friendly tailors Bindle and Keep. The film features her sister and focuses on the experiences that queer and transgender people have when getting fitted for suits.

Again and again, Dunham has used her scripts and her cameras as a forum for discussion of difficult topics. In every project she's put out into the world, Dunham has highlighted the messy, uncomfortable, embarrassing, and awkward. She has put bodies on display. Her characters have dealt with harassment and assault. In the final season of *Girls*, Hannah Horvath considers an abortion. And in her own book, *Not That Kind of Girl*, Dunham describes her own encounters with sexual assault. Over and over again, she has used her own voice to amplify the voices of others, and she continues to work to make sure the voices of women, immigrants, LGBTQ individuals, and others are heard. She has said, "You might as well advocate for the things you strongly believe in. To me, that's the only thing that gives meaning to celebrity."[13]

My sister Grace coming out as a gay woman at age seventeen was a huge turning point for me in my understanding of the issues facing LGBTQ people. We were raised in an environment—the art world of downtown Manhattan—where no one hid their sexual orientation, and a common question from four-year-old me was "Mom, are those ladies gay together?" I was always very jealous of any child who had two dads. And because of our parents' deeply held commitment to acceptance and equality, my sister's process of coming to terms with her sexuality was as angst-free as anything involving sex can really be. She was assured by the adults in her life that she was not only accepted, but adored for who she is. I am so happy that this is the way she was able to enter the world as a woman and an LGBTQ person.[14]

CHAPTER SIX

Recognition and Future Plans

Even though Dunham's biggest success to date, *Girls*, ended in 2017, she did not close the door on her life in the spotlight. After six seasons of the show, Dunham went out on a high note. In 2013, the show received the Golden Globe for Best Television Series, Comedy or Musical, and Dunham herself received the Golden Globe for Best Actress in a Television Series, Comedy or Musical. Additionally, the show and Dunham were nominated for multiple Emmy

Taking a break from screenwriting, Dunham wrote *Not That Kind of Girl*, a full-length memoir.

Awards, Critics' Choice Television Awards, and more. It enjoyed over five years of attention from viewers, much of it positive. Throughout her time with *Girls*, Dunham remained active in other forms of media—she published essays, appeared in magazines, and more. In 2014, right in the middle of her show's prime, Dunham took on a writing project that was bigger than any she'd done before, one that caused her to learn about herself, become vulnerable, and let those vulnerable parts of herself be read by fans (and enemies) across the world.

Not That Kind of Girl

In 2014, Random House published Dunham's book of essays, which was also, at its core, a memoir. A memoir is a record of events written from personal knowledge. It differs from autobiography in that a memoir doesn't often move in chronological order and doesn't usually focus so heavily on dates, facts, and research. Instead, a memoir might focus on just one period or event in a person's life, and it might take a few more liberties with memory and narrative. Dunham's memoir, for its part, spans from the early days of her childhood to the present years, though she isn't militant about chronology and transitions back and forth easily between stories of childhood, adolescence, and young adulthood. Titled *Not That Kind of Girl: A Young Woman Tells You What She's "Learned,"* the book is, indeed, a passionate and comedic telling of all the things that Dunham was taught, or taught herself, over the course of her life.

Tenderly dedicated to Nora Ephron, Dunham's late friend and mentor, the memoir contains lists, essays, and emails, all in an effort to convey stories about her life and about the lives of her family members, friends, and lovers. It is part advice book and part tell-all about her own experiences. According to Dunham, this particular project was inspired by Helen Gurley Brown's *Having It All*, a title published in 1982 that gave powerful, if often ridiculous and demeaning, advice to women. The advice that Dunham gives in her own book, such as a list of "Fifteen Things I've Learned from my Mother" and the essay "This Is Supposed to Be Fun? Making the Most of Your Education," is funny and less provocative than one might expect, especially coming from a woman who has produced her share of edgy material for the screen and page. Some sections feature classic Dunham oversharing, such as one called "Sharing Concerns: My Worst Email Ever, with Footnotes," that does include an excessive number of detailed footnotes. "Therapy and Me," "Guide to Running Away," and "My Top Ten Health Concerns" all plunge the reader right inside Dunham's own anxious mind. She never gets tired of sharing, and audiences are interested—her book spent time on the *New York Times* best seller list, and she made millions of dollars on it, both through the initial sale of the rights and through book sales. It came out in paperback in 2015.

Reviews of the book were decidedly mixed, with some enjoying her distinct voice, earnestness, and honesty, while others tired quickly of her navel-gazing and anxiety. But it remains a favorite with celebrities, friends, and fans of Dunham's. The book includes blurbs from notables like David Sedaris, Miranda July, and even Judy Blume. Of course, reviews, re-reviews, and reviews of the reviews abound online, but Dunham hasn't allowed anyone's criticism to stop her from writing. In May 2016, she dropped a surprise fifty-six-page chapbook called *Is It Evil Not to Be Sure?* The limited-release title, which completely sold out online within twenty-four hours, is a collection of Dunham's personal journals. The book profits benefited Girls Write Now, a mentoring/writing program. Dunham said she had "always believed that women chronicling their own lives, even (or especially) at their most mundane, is a radical act."[1] By supporting organizations that empower young women to write, Dunham encourages these radical acts to spread and grow, and she hasn't stopped committing acts of her own. In 2015, Dunham started to make plans for the writing project that would follow the success of *Girls.* This project would, ideally, help even more women chronicle their lives, speak up, and speak out about the things that are important to them.

Lenny

Dunham first had the idea for Lenny Letter while on tour for *Not That Kind of Girl.* After meeting with and listening to the stories of hundreds of young, female millennials, Dunham began to feel the need for a new type of community, a unique place online for women to produce and discover content. She began to discuss the idea with Jenni Konner, her longtime creative partner, best friend, and *Girls* show runner. After a few months of tinkering, Konner and Dunham released the first issue of Lenny, a weekly online newsletter, delivered both to email inboxes and posted on a website. The site bills itself as "The best from Lena Dunham and Jenni Konner in feminism, style, politics, friendship, and more," and that is, for the most part, what Lenny offers. The simple email newsletter, which premiered in October 2015 and blasts out to inboxes twice a week, features essays, interviews, artwork, and advice. The content covers a wide range of topics: gender, the workplace, relationships, politics, fashion. It's all there. And it's not just there, but it's written by women, for women. The first Lenny interview was a one-on-one with Hillary Clinton. Discussions with Jennifer Lawrence (about the gender wage gap) and Alicia Keys (about not wearing makeup) would follow.

Lenny's success has been fast-paced, and business-news outlets such as Fortune and FastCompany have picked up on that success, profiling Dunham, Konner, and their flourishing business. Lenny is a business—it has a CEO, Konner's ex-husband, Benjamin Cooley—and it is, slowly but surely, making money. Hearst Media retains the rights to distribute the newsletter, promote it, and work with advertisers. Since starting the newsletter,

Dunham and Konner have partnered with Random House to create a Lenny imprint, or trade name, under which its first two books were due out in 2017. Lenny has also expanded into a **podcast**, *Women of the Hour*, which is currently in its second season. In addition to the digital media platforms and publishing arm, Lenny Letter also operates a merchandise wing. On the "Shop" section of the website, you can find everything from Lenny-branded sweatshirts to nail wraps and incense holders. Lenny isn't meant for a specific type of woman—it hopes to provide content that nearly any and every woman can find valuable. Spurning the quick lists and visual slideshows of other websites, Lenny specializes in the long-form essay, story, and interview, exposing the reader to "meatier" content than might be the norm elsewhere on the internet. In this way, Dunham and Konner show respect for and trust in their readers; they expect them to read and come to their own conclusions, even if their feedback is negative.

Just as she has since *Tiny Furniture*, Dunham continues to deal with internet trolls and "haters," who will jump on any reason to criticize her work. There has been some negativity directed at Lenny, but nothing over the top. For the most part, the brand has attracted people for whom the content, voice, and vehicle resonate. Soon, the team at Lenny hopes to pursue even more new avenues for the brand, including potential video content and an expanded podcast section. About the future of Lenny, Konner has said, "Our interests are pretty boundless, as is our appetite for new creative experiences. We just want to be sure that what we're creating is pushing the ball forward for women and diversity in media."[2] With their truthful, bold mix of pieces about women's health, queer issues, people of color, reproductive justice, and more, the creative minds at Lenny are committed to creating a space by women, for women, that will continue to evolve and expand into just the type of space they want—and need—the most.

Jenni and Jack

In addition to her day-to-day work on Lenny Letter and other projects, Dunham also makes time for her family, friends, and boyfriend. She currently splits her time between Brooklyn, New York, and Los Angeles, California. Whenever she was hard at work on *Girls,* Dunham shared an office with her best friend, Jenni Konner, in Los Angeles. Konner first discovered Dunham's work when she watched her film *Tiny Furniture* and felt connected to it in a deep and personal way. About that moment, she told NPR, "I felt so connected to that entitled girl who didn't know what she should be doing and was kind of lost. I just couldn't believe what an amazing voice Lena had."[3] It was Judd Apatow, Dunham's friend, who brought Konner on to work on HBO's *Girls*. On set, Konner acted as both a creative partner and mother-like figure to Dunham and the other young actresses. She watched out for them both on and off set, becoming Dunham's close confidant and business partner over the course of the show. They currently manage Lenny Letter together, and they have appeared on-screen together in interviews. For now, Konner is Dunham's go-to person, aside from her boyfriend, Jack Antonoff.

Much like Konner and Dunham's chance meeting through Judd Apatow, Dunham and Antonoff were set up on a blind date by the comedian Mike Birbiglia, Antonoff's good friend. He is a musician, a member of the popular band fun., as well as the band Bleachers. About his first date with Dunham, Antonoff has said, "I told Lena everything about my whole life, because when you really like someone, you want them to know everything about you," and since then, they haven't stopped talking.[4] They are both creative and driven, yet anxious, people, so their personalities match up well. Dunham has directed a few of Antonoff's music videos, and two of his songs can be heard in the final season of *Girls*. They don't go out much, preferring, instead, to stay home together. Since they met in 2012, both have moved up the celebrity ladder, becoming more known to the public and, because of that, choosing to stay home even more, though they make themselves very accessible on social media. Their oversharing reaches a peak point on Instagram, where one can find endless pictures of them both.

As of this writing, it isn't time for Dunham and Antonoff to get married, though they've been together for several years. For any other celebrity, the questions of "Will they or won't they get married?" would be an interesting mystery, but for Dunham, the question offers yet another sharing opportunity.

In July 2015, just a month after LGBTQ individuals were granted the right to marry legally across the entire United States, Dunham penned an essay for the *New Yorker* called "The Bride in Her Head." In her piece, Dunham rehashes the wedding fantasies of her childhood and teen years, as well as her evolving political interest in the matter. She also describes the decision to hold off on marriage until all people had the right to marry:

When I was twenty-five, I met a bespectacled musician named Jack. He had a passion for John Hughes movies and driving on the Jersey Turnpike. His belief in, and insistence on, true equality for LGBTQ citizens was no small reason why I fell in love with him, and, early in our relationship, I watched him struggle with the decision of whether or not to perform at a straight couple's wedding. He discussed the matter at length with queer friends, concerned that it might be a form of betrayal (ultimately, he was given their blessing, though he seemed fairly tortured about it anyhow). The struggle was real and raw for Jack, and so it somehow became understood, between us, that we wouldn't even consider marrying until every American had the same right.[5]

Dunham and her boyfriend, Jack Antonoff, vowed to put off their own wedding until same-sex couples could get married.

According to Dunham, she and her boyfriend declared and lived out this decision with pride, though sometimes, in private, she would mutter to Jack, "Marry me." Though she was adamant that they would not, could not, get married until everyone could marry, she looked forward to the day when all people shared the right—the day when she could begin to plan her fairytale wedding. Dunham describes the morning after the Supreme Court ruled on marriage equality: "I awoke to dozens of joyful messages from friends and family, rainbows and hearts and a sense that at least one great victory for human rights had been achieved in our lifetimes."[6] Soon after those excited messages, she started to receive a different kind of text and tweet. Friends congratulated her on her newfound opening to get married and demanded to know the date of the wedding, which they had all, apparently, been waiting to attend. Unfortunately, Antonoff and Dunham were not quite on the same page when it came to the expectation for a wedding. As the next few days unfolded, their emotions ran the gamut from anxious to disappointed to sad to relieved. The "limbo" of postponing marriage while waiting for the Supreme Court decision had allowed Antonoff and Dunham some breathing room in their relationship; once the court decided, however, they had to decide too. Dunham describes it like this: "The fact is that wanting everyone to have the right to marry and wanting to *be* married are two very different things," and she's right.[7] For now, she and Antonoff have

The Other Dunham (Grace)

As Dunham has powered ahead through her twenties and into her thirties, racking up awards, selling books, and producing films, one person has kept her tethered to her past and her childhood. Lena's sister, Grace Dunham, was born when Lena was six years old. As the two sisters grew and experienced more of their lives together, they became close. For Grace, who came out as a lesbian at age seventeen, gender is something she has always wondered about, and she is taking the time to explore it more deeply. Grace uses both "she" and "they" pronouns, and she has started to accept that she doesn't have a distinct name or label for her gender identity. For her, it lies somewhere outside of the **binary**—two distinct categories—in this case, man or woman, masculine or feminine.

While Lena originally longed to produce a show like *Girls* because she didn't feel that she or her friends were represented on television, her sister's experiences as a queer and gender-nonconforming person have forced her to think even more broadly about representation, especially in the media. No matter what changes or transitions either of them experience going forward, Lena and Grace continue to nurture a very close bond. In an interview with *PrideSource*, Lena explained how impactful her sister's openness and approach to gender expression and identity have affected her own life: "Even though I consider myself female and I have a more binary approach to my sexuality, I think that Grace's idea about expanding the definition of what 'she' can mean has really opened me up," Dunham said.[8]

Lena and Grace Dunham have remained very close over the years.

not made a final decision about marriage, at least not for their own relationship. Dunham has expressed that she is learning to enjoy living in the uncertainty of her relationship. And she still likes being a wedding guest.

What's Next?

Award-winning writer. Seasoned actress. Director. Podcaster. Producer. Onetime host of *Saturday Night Live*. Popular magazine interviewee. Activist. Lena Dunham has worn, and continues to wear, an endless supply of different hats. She dives into new challenges and roles with boundless energy, forging pathways for herself even while she is consistently questioned and harassed for her choices. Some of those questions help her to grow and change, while others just serve to pull her down. But, again and again, Dunham puts herself out there to be applauded, criticized, and everything in between. Her voice—that very unique, funny, anxious one that overshares as if her life depends on it—is hers to share.

Having wrapped up the final season of *Girls*, Dunham is looking to other projects, such as the expansion of Lenny Letter, to fill her time. A podcast, online shop, and more content have been added to Lenny Letter as its subscriber base grows. Fans don't have to worry that they've seen the last of her creative work outside of Lenny, either. Dunham has also been sharing hints about her newest project, a collection of short stories called *Best and Always*. Dunham has said that the short stories will focus, for the most part, on the complicated relationships between men and women. They could potentially feature many of the same themes— intimacy, awkwardness, disappointment, inconsistent expectations—that her other works have explored.

Dunham is also staying involved with the production company she started with Jenni Konner and Ericka Naegle—A Casual Romance Productions. The company, which has already produced *Suited* and *It's Me, Hilary: The Man Who Drew Eloise*, will continue to develop additional television and film projects. *It's Me, Hilary* is a documentary that explores the life of Hilary Knight, who illustrated the Eloise picture books for children. Even though the 2016 presidential election may have ended, Dunham certainly isn't making plans to dive out of the political sphere just yet. In January 2017, she attended the Women's March on Washington, marching with millions of other demonstrators across the country to show her support for women's rights. For Dunham, the march was also a physical victory. At the time, she was just beginning to recover from multiple surgeries she'd had related to her endometriosis, a painful condition that she has dealt with since the age of twelve but that went undiagnosed until her late twenties. In perhaps her most recent moment of spotlight, Dunham appeared on the February 2017 cover of *Glamour* magazine alongside her *Girls* costars. *Glamour* chose not to retouch the image of Dunham, though the cellulite on her thigh is on full display.

For those who are interested in her ideas, her body, her medical happenings, her creative projects, and her personal history, Lena Dunham will surely continue to share. An open book, she leads other young women and men to the joys and sorrows, the highs and lows, the successes and pitfalls of sharing oneself, one's life, and one's voice with the world.

Timeline

2010

Tiny Furniture premieres at SXSW.

2008

She graduates from Oberlin College in Ohio.

2006

Dunham releases her first short film, titled *Pressure*.

Lena Dunham is born in New York City.

1986

Dunham makes *Open the Door* and *The Fountain*.

2007

Delusional Downtown Divas web series premieres online. *Creative Nonfiction* premieres at South by Southwest (SXSW).

2009

Girls makes its debut on HBO.

2012

2015

Dunham cofounds Lenny Letter, an online newsletter and website, with Jenni Konner.

2013

Dunham takes home two Golden Globes: one for her acting in *Girls* and one for her work behind the scenes.

2017

Girls concludes its sixth and final season on HBO. Dunham attends the Women's March on Washington.

Dunham's memoir, *Not That Kind of Girl*, is released by Random House.

2014

Dunham coproduces *Suited,* a documentary featuring her sister, Grace Dunham.

2016

SOURCE NOTES

Chapter 1

1. Lena Dunham, *Not That Kind of Girl: A Young Woman Tells You What She's "Learned"* (New York: Random House, 2014), 159.

2. Lena Dunham, "First Love," *New Yorker*, August 13, 2012, http://www.newyorker.com/magazine/2012/08/13/first-love-3.

3. Dunham, *Not That Kind of Girl*, 148.

4. Meghan Daum, "Lena Dunham Is Not Done Confessing," *New York Times*, September 10, 2014, https://www.nytimes.com/2014/09/14/magazine/lena-dunham.html?_r=0#.

5. Dunham, *Not That Kind of Girl*, 164.

6. Lena Dunham, "Why I'm on Team Weirdo for Life," *Seventeen*, April 23, 2015, http://www.seventeen.com/life/advice/a30244/lena-dunham-never-be-regular.

7. Maude Apatow, "Crack Your Brain Wide Open: An Interview with Lena Dunham," *Rookie*, October 27, 2014, http://www.rookiemag.com/2014/10/lena-dunham-interview.

8. Rebecca Mead, "Downtown's Daughter," *New Yorker*, November 15, 2010, http://www.newyorker.com/magazine/2010/11/15/downtowns-daughter.

9. Dunham, "First Love."

10. Ibid.

Chapter 2

1. L. V. Anderson, "The Mini-Completist: Lena Dunham," *Slate*, April 2, 2012, http://www.slate.com/blogs/ browbeat/2012/04/02/lena_dunham_s_the_fountain_tight_ shots_and_other_early_work_everything_the_filmmaker_ directed_before_girls_and_tiny_furniture.html.

2. Jada Yuan, "Almost Famous," *New York Magazine*, August 16, 2009, http://nymag.com/arts/art/features/58305.

3. Ibid.

4. Scott Macaulay, "Creative Nonfiction's Lena Dunham by Alicia Van Couvering," *Filmmaker*, March 18, 2009, http:// filmmakermagazine.com/804-creative-nonfictions-lena- dunham-by-alicia-van-couvering/#.WNhdEBIrLBI.

5. Ibid.

6. Adam Lee Sweeney, "Exclusive: 'Creative Nonfiction' Auteur Lena Dunham Gets Real," Film School Rejects, June 16, 2009, https://filmschoolrejects.com/exclusive-creative- nonfiction-auteur-lena-dunham-gets-real-30fc5e267467#. duglfz63d.

Chapter 3

1. Lorrie Moore, "Lena Dunham: Unwatchable in the Best Way," *New Yorker*, March 27, 2012, http://www.newyorker. com/culture/culture-desk/lena-dunham-unwatchable-in- the-best-way.

2. "Molly Ringwald + Laurie Simmons," *Studio 360*, March 31, 2016, http://www.wnyc.org/story/molly-ringwald-laurie- simmons.

3. Mead, "Downtown's Daughter."

4. Elizabeth Gumport, "Made in Manhattan," *n+1*, March 5, 2012, https://nplusonemag.com/online-only/film-review/ made-in-manhattan.

5. Mead, "Downtown's Daughter."

6. Lena Dunham, "Seeing Nora Everywhere," *New Yorker*, June 28, 2012, http://www.newyorker.com/culture/culture-desk/seeing-nora-everywhere.

7. Ibid.

8. Mead, "Downtown's Daughter."

Chapter 4

1. Philip Galanes, "Lena Dunham and Judd Apatow on 'Girls,' 'Geeks,' and Trolls," *New York Times*, February 11, 2017, https://www.nytimes.com/2017/02/11/fashion/lena-dunham-and-judd-apatow-on-girls-geeks-and-trolls.html.

2. Lacey Rose, "'Girls': Read Lena Dunham's Original Pitch for the Show," *Hollywood Reporter*, February 6, 2017, http://www.hollywoodreporter.com/live-feed/girls-read-lena-dunhams-original-pitch-show-972037.

3. Terry Gross, "Lena Dunham Addresses Criticism Aimed at 'Girls,'" NPR, May 7, 2012, http://www.npr.org/templates/transcript/transcript.php?storyId=152183865.

4. Emily Nussbaum, "It's Different for 'Girls,'" *New York Magazine*, March 25, 2012, http://nymag.com/nymag/features/girls-lena-dunham-2012-4.

5. Terry Gross, "Lena Dunham on Sex, Oversharing, and Writing About Lost 'Girls,'" NPR, September 29, 2014, http://www.npr.org/templates/transcript/transcript.php?storyId=352276798.

6. Josh Duboff, "Lena Dunham Says Reaction to *Girls* Pregnancy Plotline Is an 'Interesting Litmus Test,'" *Vanity Fair*, March 16, 2017, http://www.vanityfair.com/hollywood/2017/03/lena-dunham-girls-pregnancy-plot-line-reaction.

7. Anna Silman, "The *Girls* Pregnancy Plotline Says More About Us Than It Does About Hannah Horvath," *Cut*, March 24, 2017, http://nymag.com/thecut/2017/03/girls-pregnancy-says-more-about-us-than-it-does-about-hannah-horvath.html.

8. Jessica Pressler, "Lena Dunham the Activist," *Elle*, January 27, 2015, http://www.elle.com/culture/celebrities/a26409/lena-dunham-profile.

Chapter 5

1. Pressler, "Lena Dunham the Activist."
2. Liz Meriwether, "The Politics of Lena Dunham," *Vulture*, July 2016, http://www.vulture.com/2016/07/lena-dunham-dnc-c-v-r.html.
3. Ibid.
4. Lena Dunham, "Today—and Everyday—Commit to Fighting for Immigrant Women," LinkedIn, March 8, 2017, https://www.linkedin.com/pulse/today-everyday-commit-fighting-immigrant-women-lena-dunham.
5. Margaret Hartmann, "Lena Dunham Discusses 'First Time' Voting in Obama Ad, Enrages Conservatives," *New York Magazine*, October 25, 2012, http://nymag.com/daily/intelligencer/2012/10/lena-dunham-talks-first-time-in-obama-ad.html.
6. Lena Dunham, "Don't Agonize, Organize," Lenny Letter, November 11, 2016, http://www.lennyletter.com/politics/a608/dont-agonize-organize.
7. Ibid.
8. Ibid.
9. Eliana Dockterman, "Lena Dunham: 'I'm Not Interested in Defining Any Other Woman's Feminism,'" *Time*, January 18, 2017, http://time.com/4637206/lena-dunham-planned-parenthood-abortion.
10. Ibid.
11. Pressler, "Lena Dunham the Activist."
12. Simon Hattenstone, "Lena Dunham: 'People Called Me Fat and Hideous, and I Lived,'" *Guardian*, January 11, 2014, https://www.theguardian.com/culture/2014/jan/11/lena-dunham-called-fat-hideous-and-i-lived.

13. Dockterman, "Lena Dunham: 'I'm Not Interested in Defining Any Other Woman's Feminism.'"

14. Bennett Marcus, "Lena Dunham on Her Sister's Coming Out," *Vanity Fair*, April 8, 2014, http://www.vanityfair.com/style/2014/04/lena-dunham-point-foundation-honors.

Chapter 6

1. Michael Schaub, "Lena Dunham Surprises Fans with New Book Containing Excerpts from Her Diary," *Los Angeles Times*, May 17, 2016, http://www.latimes.com/books/jacketcopy/la-et-jc-lena-dunham-new-book-20160517-snap-story.html.

2. Gwen Moran, "How Lena Dunham's Budding Empire Breaks Every Rule of Business," *Fortune*, June 22, 2016, http://fortune.com/2016/06/22/lena-dunham-lenny.

3. Audie Cornish, "Meet Jenni Konner, the Off-Screen 'Grown Up' Who Helped Make 'Girls,'" NPR, March 24, 2017, http://www.npr.org/templates/transcript/transcript.php?storyId=520824854.

4. Jada Yuan, "Why Jack Antonoff Is a Pop Star Even a Mother Could Love," *Vulture*, June 18, 2014, http://www.vulture.com/2014/06/jack-antonoff-solo-album-bleachers.html.

5. Lena Dunham, "The Bride in Her Head," *New Yorker*, July 10, 2015, http://www.newyorker.com/culture/cultural-comment/the-bride-in-her-head.

6. Ibid.

7. Ibid.

8. Chris Azzopardi, "Lena Dunham Talks Subverting Hollywood Gender Norms, Why She Calls Jack Antonoff Her 'Partner' and the Influence of Her Sister's Queerness," *PrideSource*, June 9, 2016, http://www.pridesource.com/article.html?article=76876.

GLOSSARY

affluence Wealth, privilege.

apex A high point or climax.

assimilate To absorb into the traditions or customs of a popular culture or group.

autobiographical Dealing with the writer's own life.

Bechdel test A three-part test that challenges movies to have at least two named female characters, have those characters talk to each other, and cause those characters to talk about something other than a man.

binary Two distinct categories.

cult following A particular section of society that deems something fashionable, enjoyable, and popular.

domestic Of or relating to the running of the home.

feminist Someone adhering to a set of political beliefs born out of the idea that women should have certain fundamental rights and equality.

improvisation Creating spontaneously, or without preparation, in music or drama.

insinuation A suggestion of something bad.

lampoon Publicly criticize.

millennial A category for people born between the early 1980s and 2004, immediately following generation X.

mumblecore A film genre characterized by low-budget production, improvisation, naturalistic dialogue, and a focus on the relationships of young adults.

obsessive-compulsive disorder An anxiety disorder marked by unwanted and repeated thoughts, feelings, ideas, or behaviors that make someone feel driven to do or think something.

pervade Present and apparent throughout.

podcast A digital audio file that is available for downloading to a computer.

polarizing Causing a group, often of people or opinions, to separate into opposing groups.

privilege Special rights or advantages granted to a specific person or group of people.

rough cut An unfinished version of a movie, put together with minimal editing.

satirical Using irony, sarcasm, or ridicule to expose someone or something that is foolish, weak, or bad.

viral Characteristic of a video that is shared widely and rapidly on the internet.

workshop A type of class, often for writers or artists, wherein students read each other's creative work and then make comments in a group.

FURTHER INFORMATION

Books

Dunham, Lena. *Not That Kind of Girl: A Young Woman Tells You What She's "Learned."* New York: Random House, 2014.

Johnston, Kelly. *Lena Dunham: A Biography.* CreateSpace Publishing, 2017.

Schatz, Kate. *Rad American Women A–Z: Rebels, Trailblazers, and Visionaries Who Shapes Our History … and Our Future!* San Francisco: City Lights Books, 2015.

Websites

Growing Up in Therapy
http://www.newyorker.com/magazine/2014/09/01/difficult-girl

In this essay for the *New Yorker*, Lena Dunham shares her childhood experiences with mental health, anxiety, and therapy.

Laurie Simmons
http://www.lauriesimmons.net

The professional website of Lena Dunham's mother, Laurie Simmons, where you can find her art, her writing, and her photographs of tiny furniture.

Lenny Letter
http://www.lennyletter.com/

The brainchild of Lena Dunham and Jennifer Konner, Lenny Letter compiles essays, stories, and art.

***Rookie* Magazine Interview with Lena Dunham**
http://www.rookiemag.com/2014/10/lena-dunham-interview

In this interview, Lena Dunham sits down with Maude Apatow, Judd Apatow's teenage daughter, to talk about life, films, television, and high school.

Women of the Hour
https://soundcloud.com/womenofthehour

Episodes of Lena Dunham's podcast, *Women of the Hour with Lena Dunham*, can be found here.

Video

The History of 100 Years of Women's Health Care
http://www.lennyletter.com/politics/a690/100-years

This animated short film, produced by Lena Dunham, recounts the history of Planned Parenthood in honor of the organization's hundredth birthday.

BIBLIOGRAPHY

Apatow, Maude. "Crack Your Brain Wide Open: An Interview with Lena Dunham." *Rookie*, October 27, 2014. http://www.rookiemag.com/2014/10/lena-dunham-interview.

Daum, Meghan. "Lena Dunham Is Not Done Confessing." *New York Times*, September 10, 2014. https://www.nytimes.com/2014/09/14/magazine/lena-dunham.html?_r=0#.

Dix, Peyton. "Lena Dunham's Last Chance." *Outline*, March 27, 2017. https://theoutline.com/post/1308/lena-dunhams-girls-season-6.

Dockterman, Eliana. "Lena Dunham: 'I'm Not Interested in Defining Any Other Woman's Feminism.'" *Time*, January 18, 2017. http://time.com/4637206/lena-dunham-planned-parenthood-abortion.

Dunham, Lena. "Difficult Girl." *New Yorker*, September 1, 2014. http://www.newyorker.com/magazine/2014/09/01/difficult-girl.

———. "Don't Agonize, Organize." Lenny Letter, November 11, 2016. http://www.lennyletter.com/politics/a608/dont-agonize-organize.

———. "First Love." *New Yorker*, August 13, 2012. http://www.newyorker.com/magazine/2012/08/13/first-love-3.

———. *Not That Kind of Girl: A Young Woman Tells You What She's "Learned."* New York: Random House, 2014.

———. "Seeing Nora Everywhere." *New York Times*, June 28, 2012. http://www.newyorker.com/culture/culture-desk/seeing-nora-everywhere.

———. *Tiny Furniture.* Criterion Collection, 2012.

———. "Today—and Everyday—Commit to Fighting for Immigrant Women." LinkedIn, March 8, 2017. https://www.linkedin.com/pulse/today-everyday-commit-fighting-immigrant-women-lena-dunham.

———. "Why I'm on Team Weirdo for Life." *Seventeen*, April 23, 2015. http://www.seventeen.com/life/advice/a30244/lena-dunham-never-be-regular.

Gross, Terry. "Lena Dunham Addresses Criticism Aimed at 'Girls.'" NPR, May 7, 2012. http://www.npr.org/templates/transcript/transcript.php?storyId=152183865.

———. "Lena Dunham on Sex, Oversharing, and Writing About Lost 'Girls.'" NPR, September 29, 2014. http://www.npr.org/templates/transcript/transcript.php?storyId=352276798.

Gumport, Elizabeth. "Made in Manhattan," *n+1*, March 5, 2012. https://nplusonemag.com/online-only/film-review/made-in-manhattan.

Hattenstone, Simon. "Lena Dunham: 'People Called Me Fat and Hideous, and I Lived.'" *Guardian*, January 11, 2014. https://www.theguardian.com/culture/2014/jan/11/lena-dunham-called-fat-hideous-and-i-lived.

Karni, Annie, "Hillary Clinton Sits for Interview with Lena Dunham." *Politico*, September 24, 2015. http://www.politico.com/story/2015/09/hillary-clinton-lena-dunham-interview-213990.

Macaulay, Scott. "Creative Nonfiction's Lena Dunham by Alicia Van Couvering." *Filmmaker*, March 18, 2009. http://filmmakermagazine.com/804-creative-nonfictions-lena-dunham-by-alicia-van-couvering/#.WNhdEBIrLBI.

Malle, Chloe. "Lena Dunham on the End of *Girls*, Her New Book, and the Legacy of 'Unlikeable' Women." *Vogue*,

December 14, 2016. http://www.vogue.com/article/girls-hbo-final-season-lena-dunham.

Mead, Rebecca. "Downtown's Daughter." *New Yorker*, November 15, 2010. http://www.newyorker.com/magazine/2010/11/15/downtowns-daughter.

Meriwether, Liz. "The Politics of Lena Dunham." *Vulture*, July 2016. http://www.vulture.com/2016/07/lena-dunham-dnc-c-v-r.html.

"Molly Ringwald + Laurie Simmons." *Studio 360*, March 31, 2016. http://www.wnyc.org/story/molly-ringwald-laurie-simmons.

Moore, Lorrie. "Lena Dunham: Unwatchable in the Best Way." *New Yorker*, March 27, 2012. http://www.newyorker.com/culture/culture-desk/lena-dunham-unwatchable-in-the-best-way.

Nussbaum, Emily. "It's Different for 'Girls.'" *New York Magazine*, March 25, 2012. http://nymag.com/nymag/features/girls-lena-dunham-2012-4.

Pressler, Jessica. "Lena Dunham the Activist." *Elle*, January 27, 2015. http://www.elle.com/culture/celebrities/a26409/lena-dunham-profile.

Rose, Lacey. "'Girls': Read Lena Dunham's Original Pitch for the Show." *Hollywood Reporter*, February 6, 2017. http://www.hollywoodreporter.com/live-feed/girls-read-lena-dunhams-original-pitch-show-972037.

Slonim, Jeffrey. "Lena Dunham and Gloria Steinem Rate Jack Antonoff as a Feminist-Friendly Boyfriend." *People*, April 25, 2016. http://people.com/tv/lena-dunham-boyfriend-jack-antonoff-supports-her-feminism.

Wappler, Margaret. "Lena Dunham Is Our February Cover Star." *Nylon*, January 11, 2017. http://www.nylon.com/articles/lena-dunham-nylon-february-cover.

INDEX

Page numbers in **boldface** are illustrations. Entries in **boldface** are glossary terms.

ABOUT THE AUTHOR

Kaitlyn Duling believes in the power of words to change hearts, minds, and, ultimately, actions. A poet, nonfiction author, and grant writer who grew up in Illinois, she now resides in Pittsburgh, Pennsylvania, where she works aboard a bookmobile for Reading is Fundamental Pittsburgh and helps kids learn to love to read. She knows that knowledge of the past is the key to our future and wants to make certain that all children and families have access to high-quality, relevant information. She is a feminist. This is her fourth book for Cavendish Square.